Acknowledgements

Dr A Somerville-Ford, for initiating the core of the text; Mrs Diana Aldridge, for assistance with source documents; Elliot Newman, for the cover design, for abstracting the former roads of Christchurch from the 1878 Portfield Enclosure Award and for photographic enhancements; Mr Peter Hall, for allowing access to the Coward's Marsh account book; David Eels (the expert on the De Redvers' family); Christchurch Borough Council; Brian Schollar, Terry Tuck; the late Mrs Mabel Perry and many others not otherwise separately thanked.

CW01499610

Other books by Sue Newman:

The Christchurch and Bournemouth Union Workhouse, second edition, 2000 self-published
first edition, 1994 self-published

Lives and Times of a Victorian House in Christchurch, 1989, self-published (out of print)
Christchurch in Old Picture Postcards, 1997, European Library (out of print)
Christchurch, the Archive Series, 1997, reprinted 1998, Tempus Publications

The Chain Gang, 2006 (e-book, self-published), available directly from the author

In Preparation:
The Chain Gang, in book form, renamed *Christchurch: its people and its horology, 1700-1900*

Articles by Mike Tizzard

These have frequently appeared in the Christchurch Local History Society's *Quarterly* bulletin (edited by Sue Newman), the Christchurch Antiquarians' magazines, and also for Keith Jarvis' *Excavations in Christchurch 1969-1980*.

THE CHRISTCHURCH COMMONS

HISTORY and WALKS

First published in 2007 by Natula Publications
Natula Ltd., 5 St Margarets Avenue, Christchurch, Dorset BH23 1JD

ISBN 9781897887646
© Sue Newman and Mike Tizzard 2007

A CIP catalogue record of this book is available from the British Library.

Printed by
Cpod, Trowbridge, Wiltshire.

Illustrations
Front Cover: 1898 Sales Plan of Millhams
Back Cover: Millhams Mead North

Pages 4 and 34: Courtesy of Ordnance Survey
Page 8: Courtesy of Christchurch Borough Council
Pages 12 and 14: Courtesy of Julian White
Page 20: Courtesy of Mrs M. Perry
All other illustrations from the authors' own collections

Contents

Illustrations

Illustrations (continued)

Preface

Christchurch's modern borough has hundreds of acres of open spaces, a considerable proportion of which is common land yet relatively unknown, and certainly not featured in any depth in published works.

This book attempts to redress this and to bring these delightful and ancient, and accessible common lands to wider attention and greater public enjoyment. We have confined the study to those commons for which the inhabitants of the Old Borough of the town had rights, thus leaving others to investigate the numerous other commons of the modern borough, such as Burton Common, Winkton Common, Barlins, and a host of tiny and possibly lost commons, such as Blackwater Common and various Poors Commons.

It is not a definitive work: much more could have been added, and it is to be hoped that it will be a starting point for further research and interest. It is intended to provide a detailed history as far as it can be ascertained and without descending into tedious detail, about each common, together with suggestions about how to explore them on foot, for they appear to be an untapped resource for leisure and tranquillity in an increasingly built-up modern borough.

The maps used are, for historic and copyright reasons, not current, but contemporary with the commons when they made a highly valued and important contribution to the local economy, which was still essentially a rural one. Furthermore, the boundaries of many commons appear never to have been defined: the outlines provided are by no means definitive (even Dorset County Council could not provide those) but are certainly broadly correct.

The authors, Sue Newman and Mike Tizzard, have worked together in local history for many years, collaborating on projects, initiatives and investigations, and sharing research. Mike has been involved on a practical and research level in history, and archaeology in particular, since boyhood, and took part in some of the town digs in the 1980s, as well as numerous digs elsewhere. He has also made an extensive study of the town documents, which date back to medieval times, and of the 1844 tithe map, which defines each plot of land in the parish and its ownership. He is currently chairman of The Christchurch Antiquarians. Sue took up local history research on coming to Christchurch in 1979, and has published six books on the town and many magazine articles, as well as playing an executive role in various societies with the objective of preserving and exploring the history and heritage of the town. She has also contributed extensively to the local and county council's consultation papers and policy documents on planning and the built environment.

The authors were also the principal creators of the Millennium Trail: the town's 18 blue plaques and their accompanying guide.

We trust this joint publication will enable the commons to remain unviolated, to be recognised as the essential fabric of the town's history and, most importantly, provide new opportunities for recreation. For those who enjoy walking, bird watching, wild flowers and rural scenery: this is for you.

NB: This is written from sources as closely researched as feasible. It may generate debate. We hope that it does. And be aware – just because something appears in print, it ain't necessarily so! Although every effort has been made to be accurate, any mistakes are regrettable and we accept responsibility for them.

This is a subject which has not previously been addressed. This book draws on many sources to produce a work which makes serious inroads into this deficiency. We hope it creates interest from which further research could be done to shed even more light on our commons heritage.

The Countryside Code

Please follow the code when following the walks. The code asks you to:

Respect the life and work of the countryside;
Guard against all risk of fire (especially relevant to Town Common);
Fasten all gates;
Keep dogs under close control;
Keep to public paths where applicable;
Use stiles and gates where appropriate;
Take your litter home;
Help to keep all water clean;
Protect wildlife, plants and trees;
Make no unnecessary noise.

Thank you

Opposite:
The extent of the commons extrapolated onto a 1930s guidebook map, using the tithe book as a source. This does not include an area of Bernard's Mead to the east of Barrack Road currently included by Christchurch Borough Council

Introduction

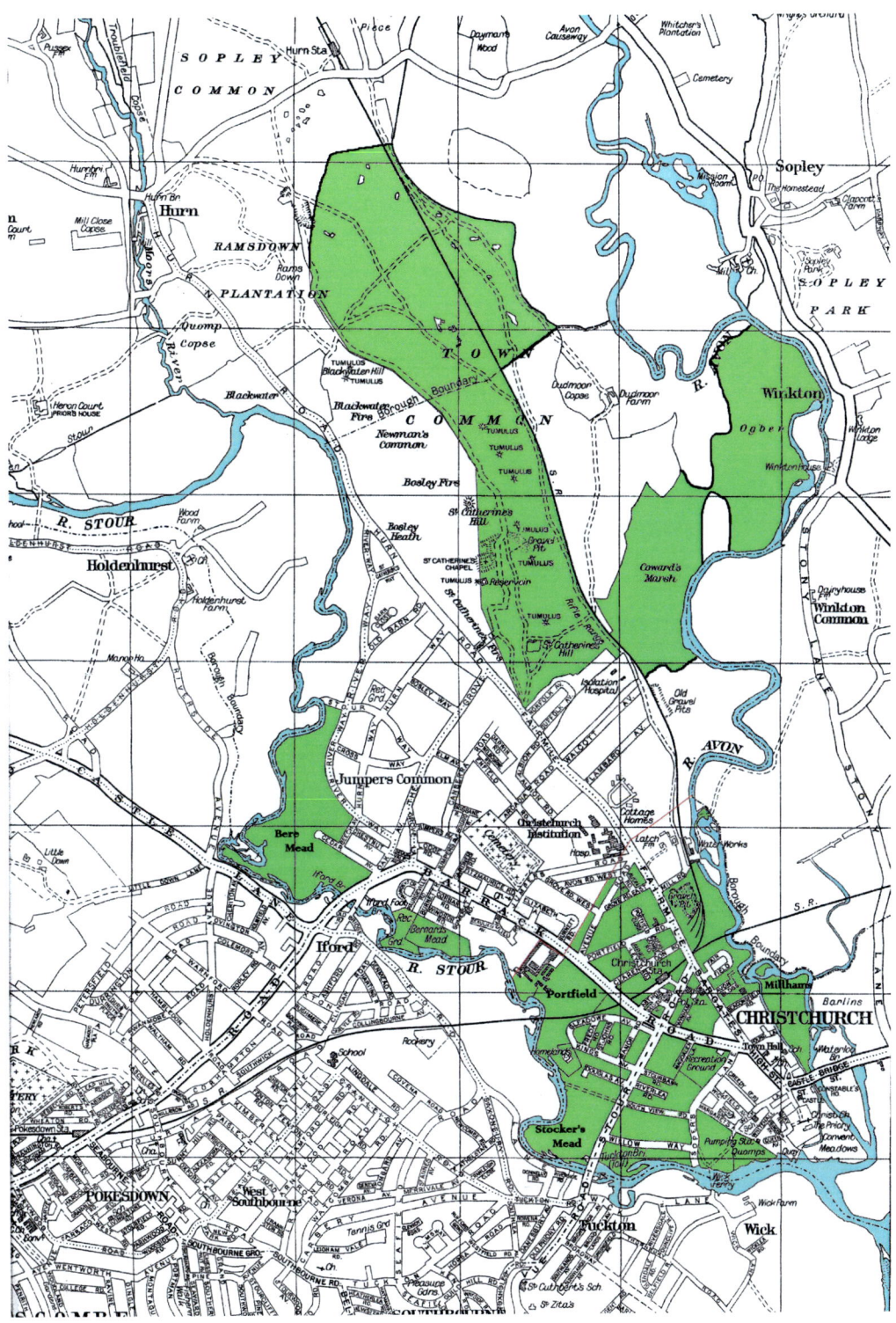

In 1681, only a few years after the end of the long and bloody English Civil Wars, the principal inhabitants of the ancient borough of Christchurch met in the Court House of the Manor of Christchurch-Twyneham, adjacent to the Priory Church, owners of that manor. The purpose of the meeting was to hold a Court Leet at which they reaffirmed their ancient rights in:

'Our Commons of Turf Delph, Coward's Marsh, Gravel Pits and Comps (Quomps) our free commons for ever, pertaining to our tenements.'

Turf Delph is the old name for Town Common, and Comps is, of course, Quomps. The jurors next presented the 'Lammas' lands of Ogber and Millhams, both open from that feast day through to 'Candlemas', or 14 February. Next came a further list of smaller areas of Lammas lands: Cowslip Mead, Plowman's Mead, Dashwin's Mead, Tufton (aka Tuckton) Corner and Merritt's Mead (the charmingly named Cowslip Mead is better known by its later name of Stocker's Mead). The next presentment was of a list of enclosures, which those attending wished to make clear they still regarded themselves as having common rights in: Markett's Close, Trim's Close, both in the 'West Marsh' (the quay and westwards), and Dashwin's Close, Colgell's Close (located on the east of Bargates), Chappell's Close and Common Close in Portfield, which *'ought to be laid open yearly at the breach of the field* (i.e. Portfield) *according to our ancient custom'*.

Over a century and a half later, the same declaration was made at a Court Leet held for another of the three Christchurch manors, that of the Manor of the Borough, adding two other unauthorised enclosures of Portfield – Collin's Close and Coffin's Close, plus Lyte's Mead, adjacent to Stocker's Mead. It is obvious that these extensive commons were vital to the livelihoods of the populace of the town, and the rights associated with them of such value that their erosion would be fiercely resisted, as the story of the Christchurch commons demonstrates over the centuries, over and over again. The two presentments prove that the commoners of two manors, that of the Borough and of the (Priory) Manor of Christchurch-Twyneham, shared these common rights.

The 'ancient custom' referred to at these Courts Leet was already of such antiquity that the origins were lost in the mists of time; some of the rights were known as 'customary' - meaning that they were largely an oral tradition, unsubstantiated by documentation, a fact which weighed heavily against commoners when the vast arable area of Portfield was enclosed in 1878. Other rights were by prescription, or charter, although the original charter may have been lost: an example of the latter is Stocker's Mead, granted by Baldwin de Redvers, later the 7th Earl of Devon, c.1258/9, to the Burgesses, along with Bernard's (also known as Burnett's) Mead and Bere (also known as Bure) Mead. That grant was restricted, though, to what is known as the aftershare, or the pasture in the meadow after the hay has been gathered. And the burgesses had to pay an annual rent of 30 shillings for this privilege.

Before continuing, a word about the ancient festivals of Lammas and Candlemas, the roots of which go deep into the Celtic era but became absorbed into the Christian rituals.

Lammas, until the change of the calendar in 1752 - when ten days were lost and the year started on 1 January and not, as before, on 25 March, known as Lady Day – was held on 1 or 2 August. It marked both the beginning of the harvest and the first baking of the bread from it (Lammas may be derived from 'loaf mass'). Candlemas, formerly on 2 February, is the celebration of forty days since the birth of Jesus and of the ritual purification of the Virgin Mary, but, more anciently, it was part of the solar calendar by which both agriculture and ritual or religious events were marked. Candlemas was half way between the winter solstice and the spring equinox: thus, halfway through winter. Throughout this text you will notice two dates given for these feast days, depending on the date of the source used.

It would appear that the commons arose as a result of the Conquest, or were codified at that time; the boundary of the Old Borough being the extent of the town or burgh in the 1086 Domesday Survey. By parcelling out the land into manors, large areas of less fertile land were regarded as 'waste' of the manor, or unused at the time; whilst other areas of land were enclosed and cultivated in the familiar strip system and the fallow land became regarded as common pasture by freeholders and 'copyholders' of the manor. No discussion about common rights can avoid a modicum of understanding of the Christchurch manors, so an extremely brief overview follows.

The main manor was the huge one of the Manor of Christchurch, including within it thousands of acres extending towards the New Forest and including the Liberty of Westover (modern Bournemouth). All other manors were subsidiary to this manor, and the Lord of the Manor of Christchurch was the Overlord of these lesser manors. The Manor of the Borough, to which many of the common rights described refer, was a lesser manor and, confusingly, until 1791 in the same ownership as the main manor, in which year Sir George Ivison Tapps sold it to Sir George Rose, and in 1863, his son Sir George Henry Rose, sold it to Lord Malmesbury. The third manor was that of the Priory, known as the Manor of Christchurch-Twyneham, with property dotted about the town and neighbourhood. Since 1830 this has been in the ownership of the Tapps/Gervis/Meyrick family, as has the main manor since 1708.

The common rights in Town Common, Coward's Marsh and Quomps are shared between the two lesser manors, but therefore ultimately belong to the main manor. The Manor of the Borough alone was granted the common rights to Bere, Bernard's and Stocker's Meads. (The income was in part paid to the landowner, and part used to keep in repair property belonging to the Old Corporation and maintaining the commons.) It is for these reasons that the ownership of most of the commons, and the exact nature of the rights they are subject to, are deeply steeped in complex legal and historical twists and turns which have given rise to so many disputes over the centuries.

In this somewhat organic fashion, the rights evolved, but as they arose within the feudal system they were attached to the properties within the manor, rather than to individuals. It is also important to note that the commons were and are still owned by one or more persons, and do not necessarily belong to those who have rights over them.

The town (Old Corporation) documents reveal so much about the careful administration of the commons. Many examples of this are recorded, but one example is from October 1655: *'In beer and cakes, and points when we viewed the bounds of our common, 5s 4d'*. The townspeople regularly checked the boundaries and condition of the commons, so economically vital were they through the ages.

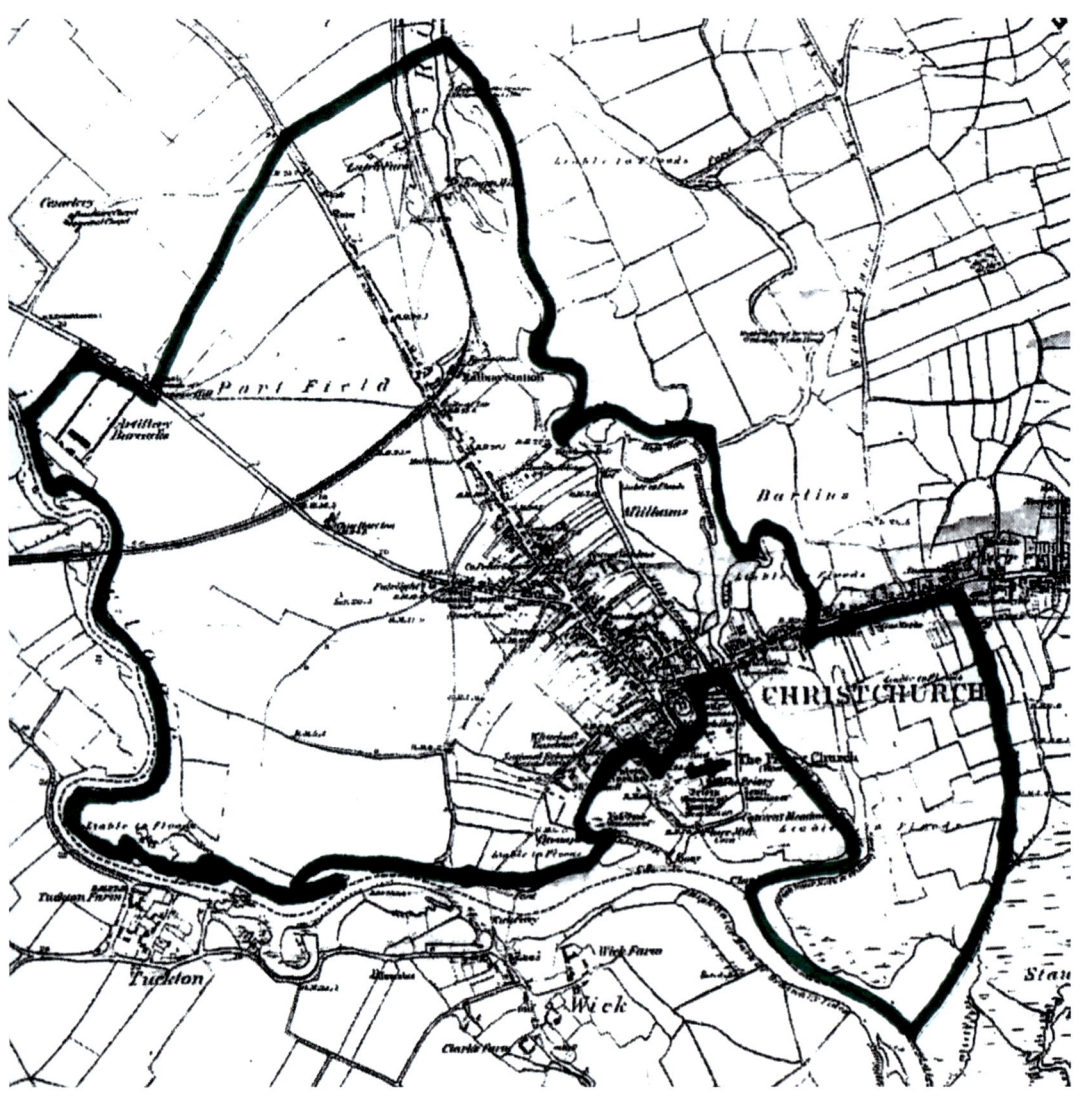

Boundary of the Old Borough, based on OS 1870

Various types of rights applied to individual commons, the most important of which was common of pasture. This was limited, naturally, to 'commonable' animals, i.e. cows, horses and sheep, which could either plough or manure the land, but not geese, goats or pigs. All the Christchurch commons were subject to rights of pasture. This right could and was often limited, being available only part of the year in most cases, and restricted to a set number of animals, or certainly no more than the commoner would be able to support on his own patch of land during those times when the commons were closed for pasture - in theory. Another extremely valuable right was that of turbary, or the right to cut turf for fuel: this was restricted to taking only enough for the commoner's own use; it was important to the survival of the common that economic exploitation was prevented. Turf burnt slowly in the hearth and was thus cheap as a fuel source for cooking and heating. Town Common has rights of turbary. The right to estover meant that the commoner could remove undergrowth - again for fuel. This right, along with that of pasture, applies to Coward's Marsh. The right of soil relates to the digging of sand, stones and minerals, again for the commoner's own use: it applies to Town Common but was much abused, as will be seen later.

Eligibility for these rights was acquired by living within the boundaries of the Old Borough (see map, page 4), but several times confusion and disputes arose about the exact definition of the boundary, hard to be categoric about after centuries of alteration to the roads and fields. Yet so valuable were the rights considered to be that even in the 20th century a determined and aggrieved would-be commoner, Mr R J Maidment, took the matter to court for a ruling. He lived in Waterloo House, alongside the bridge of the same name, and the case hinged on how much of his domestic quarters were within the borough, the boundary of which went straight through the carriage arch at street level. Mr Maidment needed a fireplace within the borough, to qualify as a 'pot-boiler', or having a hearth within the borough. Even the legal brains were unable to give a certain verdict; eventually an exasperated Commoners' Committee ruled him to be outside the boundary and so ineligible.

Another point of contention was whether a new house built within the Old Borough on a plot on which no house had previously stood was entitled to these common rights. In 1867 the number of houses in the Old Borough was given (by James Druitt) as 470, almost half of which could certainly not support a cow or a horse in the winter months. The technical name for the transgression of adding a house on vacant land is 'purpresture' and that it was considered to be an outrage against commoners is vividly recounted in the section on Portfield.

The wider area of the town had other commons, applying to people living in other areas apart from the central Old Borough one: Barlins was 23 acres before the bypass was built, for those in Street Tithing (Bridge Street, Purewell etc). Other examples are Burton Common, Winkton Common and Hurn Common, but our study concentrates on the huge areas to the north-east of the town, comprised of the three separate but adjoining commons of Coward's Marsh, Ogber and Town Common (Turf Delph); plus the vast Portfield, Millhams in the town itself, and Quomps; together with the smaller commons as presented throughout the years at the Court Leets, such as Stocker's Mead.

Barlins

Some of these commons, such as Town Common, were available all year, but the majority had one main closed period, usually, though not always, coinciding. For centuries there must have been large numbers of people out and about at the opening of this common and the closing of that, moving their stock to other pasture. Whilst at no time were all the available commons closed, there were lean periods, especially in March and April, when most of them were, and the stock must have crowded on to the tiny pasture of Quomps or the somewhat ungrassy acres of Town Common during those months, or had to resort to the tenements of their owners. With possibly hundreds of cattle and horses involved, the Old Borough must have been fairly heaving with these beasts in late winter and early spring. No small wonder that the opening, or breach, of Coward's Marsh became the occasion of great celebration, no doubt one in which the newly released animals must have heartily concurred.

Before commencing the account of each common, there was one small piece of manorial property which served as a vital adjunct to the management of the commons, and it stood where the underpass to the bypass now is, at the head of Pound Lane. This was the town pound. For centuries this walled and railed enclosure was used to impound all animals straying in the town or unlawfully on the commons. It was said to have a carved stone 'M' incorporated in it, believed to be the emblem of the Montacute family, owners of the main Christchurch manor in the late 14th and early 15th centuries. This stone disappeared in 1936, as did the pound itself in 1958, once it was conveyed into the council's ownership, a piece of the fabric of medieval Christchurch of inestimable interest. Its very walls were probably built from the rubble of the 12th century bargate nearby, demolished in 1744. The authors have included it in their Millennium Trail blue plaques scheme.

Town Common (Turf Delph)

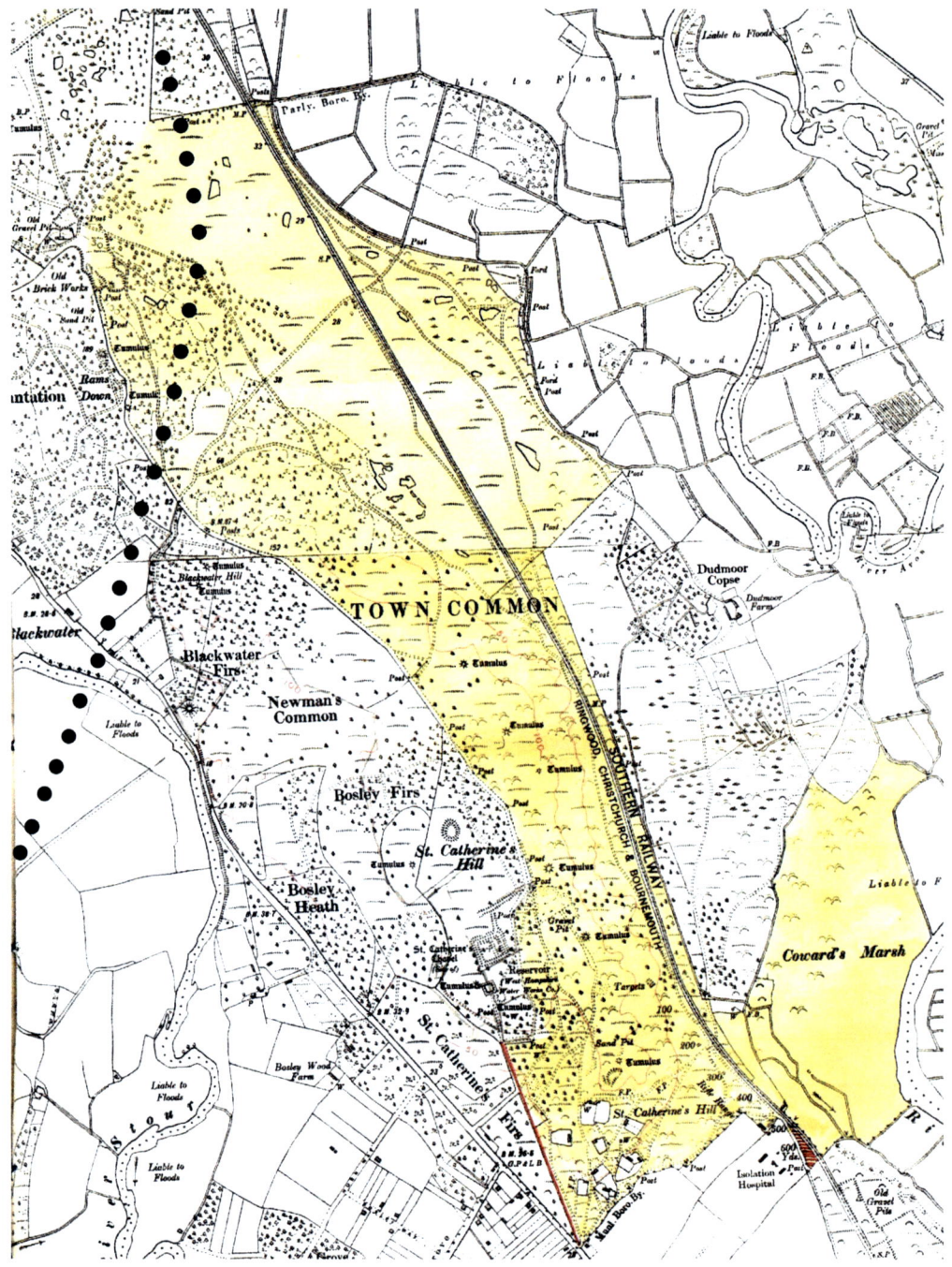

1925 revocable deed from Lord Malmesbury.
Note the curious uncertainty over the boundary on the western side where a line is drawn around the 'fort' and the chapel (see below) but not coloured in. The dotted line marks the present A338 spur road

This vast area of common land, somewhere in the region of 100 acres or more, has probably had the most contentious history of all the other local commons, yet the outcome has proved to be of great benefit to all the local people, who now have rights to roam over this beautiful area and enjoy the stunning panoramic view, a privilege which was historically only granted to the inhabitants of the Old Borough.

The original name for the common was Turf Delph. The very name implies its nature: for delph means a place from which something is dug (or delved) - and in this case it is turf.

Its boundary with Coward's Marsh was defined by a bank and ditch but since 1862 the Ringwood railway line, now disused and the track gone, runs parallel to the boundary. Town Common is part of the wider St Catherine's Hill, a total acreage of about 360. It is the common with the most rights attached to it, for they include a right to the soil, clay and gravel as well as the turf, heath and furze and the pasturage. Heath included heather, and commoners probably set up hives on this to produce honey. Clay was a constituent of cob walls, from which many Christchurch cottages were built, although few survive. Brick-making was also practised – but strictly for sale to the Old Borough inhabitants only. Town Common was also open all year, without charge, which must have been most useful in late spring when all other commons apart from the tiny area of Quomps were closed for grazing. It was certainly the traditional destination for cattle at the closing of Portfield in February.

Unfortunately, the relative rights of the landowner in the 19th century (Malmesbury) and the inhabitant householders clashed: the inhabitants were not restricting themselves to taking what they needed for their own domestic use, but actually in effect mining the ground for sand and gravel and taking it some distance away to sell it, and fiercely resisting any attempt by other legitimate commoners to obtain the same for themselves. Moreover, inhabitants from other districts outside the Old Borough, such as Blackwater and Hurn, were turning their cattle out, again in some cases actually barring the legitimate commoners from doing so, and even when they could exercise their rights very little of the sparse feed was left for their animals. In the absence of a management presence and clear set of rules such as was drawn up for Coward's Marsh, such a situation was almost bound to happen.

A notorious attempt was made by one of the Earls of Malmesbury to claim the land as his own by placing a replica, cast iron, stag on it; the furious commoners removed it by horse and cart, impounded it in the town pound (near the underpass in Pound Lane), charged an impounding fee, and even provided the 'animal' with hay and water to justify the 4d poundage charge. The attempt was foiled when the Earl's men rescued their creation by winching it out of the pound ('The Free Commons of Christchurch', *Christchurch Times* 11 April 1891 and later).

In 1859 a committee was formed to investigate the rights and report back. Whatever this report had to say, if anything, it appears to have been ineffective since only months later the outrages escalated and the letters to the press complained of green turf 'bodily removed' extensively, and, as with the sand and gravel of previous occasions, being sold out of the borough. Town Common appears to have been in the process of being steadily dismantled by one-man entrepreneurs. The letter writer pointed out that the real commoners were the poor, who did not have the means to go to the law to get redress: *'They do not like to have an iron heel to trample down their rights.'* The profit motive was plainly subverting the true purpose of common rights.

The legal status of Town Common was investigated in connection with the attempt by the Rural District Council to regulate it in 1925. There had been for some time a serious nuisance created by gypsies and from rubbish dumpers and the purpose of the attempt to regulate Town Common was to eliminate this nuisance by devising bylaws to prevent it or take action against it. Lord Malmesbury felt greatly aggrieved by the present 'lawless chaos', complaining in a letter to Herbert Druitt, that *'The commoners prefer to have any thieves and vagabonds on [the common] rather than recognise his lawful title and privileges . . . The whole neighbourhood seems to think they can just go and do what they like'*, which included by this time, cutting the trees down. The legal opinion was that whilst this common was manorial waste land, and therefore now owned by Lord Malmesbury as Lord of the Manor, his rights were severely limited by those of the commoners. Whilst the soil was vested in him, therefore so were sporting rights, mineral rights, rights to the grass, underwood, heather and timber. There was no customary right for the commoners to remove any soil or gravel. Nevertheless, the Lord had no right to take away that grass, over which commoners had grazing rights, nor remove the turf, on account of the turbary rights; but it was definitely unlawful for anyone to remove soil of any description. The Lord might grant a person the privilege of removing sand or gravel or turf, but not to the detriment of the other commoners' rights - that is to say, there had to be enough left for other legitimate users. The important point is that the rights are held in common - to both owner and commoners. Neither must damage the other's ability to exert these rights.

The Earl supported the Regulation Scheme, but such was the opposition from commoners including a petition with 600 signatories, as referred to in the discussion of Coward's Marsh, that the plan was dropped; it would have needed the support of a third of eligible commoners to have proceeded. The eventual solution was found under the 1925 Law of Property Act, whereby the public at large were granted freedom of access but no fires may be lit; this effectively excluded gypsies.

During both wars, the common was utilised by the army: in World War One for trench warfare practice, even cutting trenches, which damaged the archaeology considerably, and once again in the next world war. Matters did not stop there: the Town Planning Committee of the day had to be fended off by Lord Malmesbury in their decision to allow the Territorials to train on the hill. The operations were to include 'certain grading and *bulldozing* operations'. (Italics our own.) (Terry Tuck: Malmesbury papers.)

Town Common today remains in the ownership of the Malmesbury Estate, having been turned down by the Town Council in 1936 when it was offered to them together with all the manorial rights (on the grounds of the expense of fencing it). The major part of it is now managed by the Herpetological Conservation Trust.

A note in the Red House Museum says that James Druitt (junior) either burnt or sent for salvage the records for Turf Delph – a considerable loss to history. The following eye-witness account from the late Victorian era has therefore added value and was recalled by Robert Starks:

I am told that a lot of the land that belonged to the town has been pinched from the poor by those that got plenty. Town Common, where the poor used to get their turf and other fuel from, I am told the Lord of the Manor claimed all the rights of cutting turf etc. I cannot understand why the Lord of the Manor has got the right to collect the quit rents, as they call it, from those that have houses on the common. It appears that as the people died so the right of the property died with them, and the Lord of the Manor claimed the land and let the cottages go to ruin, so that most of the old houses are gone and the gardens are a sort of no-mans' land.

My father told me the way people used to get their own house on the common was to buy or get in some way an old wagon, a farm wagon for preference, as this was generally bigger than other vehicles. Anyway, after they had got the wagon they would build a house on it with hurdles and a chimney with bricks and clay and cover the hurdles with rushes and mud to keep the place warm and dry. Then after they had got everything ready on some moonlit night (after they had prospected around and found some plot of land to their liking) then they would get some men and horses and haul the house to the piece of ground.

Then after the house was put (where sometime or other it would be enlarged) the fire would be lit, and the pot put on, and always after the house had been permanently built the fire had to be kept burning and the pot hung over it, but during the time they were fixing the wagon most of the men were busy marking out the garden turning up a spit of turf right round the piece of ground, and, of course, in after years as the time rolled on, by throwing up the bank outside they made the plot larger. The house – by getting clay out of the plot they made mud and mixed straw or some other stuff with it and built their cottage around the old one on wheels. My father used to say it made a lot of hard work, but the women and all the family had a hand in it. Well, after they had got the roof on they dismantled the old wagon and finished the cottage at leisure, and I can assure you that most of those mud cottages was nice and warm in the winter with their big chimney corners. In those days most of the family would be in bed by seven or eight o'clock – there was no place for amusement for young people to go in the evenings, and when the dark evenings came the lads could not work out of doors. They used to go to bed and have a good night's sleep, as most of them had to be up so early.

Ingenuity, audacity, desperation, determination and fierce independence are all indicated by this remarkable description of the use of the 'waste' for home-built and humble shelters – a process which must have persisted down the centuries. The hill cottagers were a law unto themselves in many respects, and a close community of self-made outlaws.

Nevertheless, some legal framework controlled at least some of the cottage-owners. A letter of 1906 from Charles Kerley (Terry Tuck – Malmesbury papers), of Bargates, who had sublet his cottage on the common, refers to a lease of 1829 from Sir George Rose, the then Lord of the Manor, to Mr Kerley's grandfather. The house, 'simply built of green timber and mud', had only survived for so long because of the present Mr Kerley's care and attention. But he did not consider it justified to put it back in repair yet again. He refers to the original lease as being determinable on a number of 'lives': this means that the lease would have related to several consecutive people, usually three, and usually consecutive members of the same family. This is known as copyhold tenure. The rent was 1s 6d, but was increased during Mr Kerley's lifetime to £1 10s – this would be yearly. Now he was being asked for £5. The 'lives' had expired and the cottage had reverted to Lord Malmesbury. Mr Kerley had no legal arrangement with the present Lord. Refusing to sign a new and lengthy legal agreement without at least some assistance towards the cost of the repairs needed, Mr Kerley was given notice to quit. The new agreement in any case would not permit subletting.

Old cottages on St Catherine's Hill

Such was the tenuous hold these very poor people had on their self-built dwellings, which were in reality, little more than hovels when constructed.

In 1769, an intriguing new addition to the existing cottages was erected by the parish churchwardens and their Overseers of the Poor. It was a Pest House. The 18th century was an era riddled with infectious and very serious diseases, the principal killer being smallpox. Any paupers receiving parish relief on account of being too ill to maintain themselves, could or would be consigned far away from the town and the spread of the contagion, if they were considered to be a danger to the health of others. They were kept in a two-roomed cottage (presumably one room for each sex), fed and treated as best as the remedies available could provide (liquorice, pomegranate, cinnamon, malt, treacle, amongst other 'cures') and attended to by the parish surgeon. The cottage survives still on Town Common (*The Christchurch and Bournemouth Workhouse*, Sue Newman).

Walk

A typical shady woodland scene on the common

Many walks may be enjoyed merely by wandering over both Town Common and the entire St Catherine's Hill; here we describe one route which will take in most of Town Common's features and far-reaching views, and some of St Catherine's. There are many crossings and turnings: the proliferation of 'turn left' or 'turn right' instructions is unavoidable.

Warning: this is an area of exceptional wildlife interest, especially for the rare species of sand lizards which thrive on the common (90% of the remaining lizards are found on Dorset heathlands). There are also deer. Please keep your dog on a lead, and keep to the trodden paths, as straying into the vegetation not only threatens the sand lizards but wears down and erodes the vegetation.

You can reach Town Common via Marsh Lane from the small car park off Fairmile.

This spot which carries the delightful old name of Creed's Cross (*Bournemouth Echo* 26 June 1925 et al), has three tracks. Take either the extreme left-hand or the middle, main track marked St Catherine's (they eventually join up). Note the housing estate which crept up the foothillls of St Catherine's in the 1960s – controversial even at the time.

Carry on up this pathway until you soon reach a clearing: keep left, and at the next junction with a right-hand track, keep straight ahead. You will join a gravel track which you cross over and then take the right track. A ridge soon appears where you meet another track, and where you turn right (this is the track from Sandy Lane). A line of telegraph poles on your right marks the presence of the Royal Observer Corps during the Cold War period: part of a warning system now mercifully defunct. When you join another track turn left, still following the poles. Note on your left a bank and ditch system running alongside for a while.

Continue until you meet a steep, raised bank on your right. Go right. Notice a substantial and partly buried waterpipe alongside this track: this leads down from the town's first reservoir of 1905, when mains water came to the town and all the other sources, particularly wells, were superseded. The path narrows and concrete platforms have been inserted to stabilise the slope. Crossing over the concrete, and still following the poles, bear left. The path climbs onwards and becomes steep.

View from Town Common towards Southbourne, as it was around the early 20th century

At the top of the path, you will see the reservoir rather buried in vegetation on the right, and a bench in front of it from which you can pause for a while and enjoy the panoramic view you will have earned yourself. It stretches across Southbourne (you can see the distinctive pinnacles of the old water tower) and such an extensive area to the west of Southbourne that on a clear day the Purbecks are visible. Note the blue roof of Bournemouth Hospital dominating the right of the scene. Just to the left of the bench is a very low mound: one of the many Bronze Age barrows dotted around the common and in a rather sorry and depleted state.

Once sufficiently rested and having drunk in the unparalleled view, continue the walk on the same path, past dense pinewoods. The bank defining the edge of the common can be seen again by looking down the side of the steep left-hand side of the path. It appeared to be the boundary between the common and the rest of the hill until the early 19th century. The tithe map hesitatingly surrounds this area with a dotted line, and subsequent maps exclude the fort and the Roman Camp; a 'grey area' comprised of a lozenge-shaped plot called Coxes Common appears here on some maps halfway up this western edge of the huge common. The Malmesbury papers are silent on this subject – in fact they appear to have been destroyed by vandals – so we can only speculate about any change in boundary.

Where the path forks, take the right-hand one, and at the first minor track through the heather on the right-hand side, proceed to the site of the chapel first recorded in 1302, and now surrounded in a square shape by a number of banks which to the trained eye can be discerned. These banks are thought to be a Roman Signal Station (within which the chapel was later built). If this is correct, here beacons would have been lit to alert shipping or some matter of importance or act as a guide, from a vantage point not then obscured by tree growth as now.

Little remains of what may have dated back to Roman times and was certainly in use in the medieval period (further details may be explored elsewhere). The site's historical damage included its use by the Royal Horse Artillery in World War One. The chapel may have served the long-lost ancient hamlet of Rishdon (or its other spellings).

Retrace your steps as far as the main gravel path. Cross over it and turn right. The roaring traffic noise from the A338 is very intrusive at this point: the road actually bisects the common at its northerly end. Continue along this path on the edge of the hill until when you meet a 'T-junction' first one and then another reservoir comes into view to your right, replacements for the original. Turn left past the nearest of these two monuments, one cylindrical, one rectangular: shortly, on your left, a banked and ditched oval-shaped enclosure of unknown date can be seen. It has never been excavated, but demonstrates yet again the intense human activity which has taken place on the common over many centuries. Pass to the left of the latest addition to the common: two masts towering above an electrical brick-built complex. Ahead of you, you once again encounter the boundary bank of the common: turn right on the path in front of this.

Where this path bears to the right, proceed straight ahead on a branch track, to borrow railway terminology. After a short distance, near the crossroads, turn left onto another main track. Proceed over the crossroads; the bank continues on your left.

At the dip in the path, the lowest point observable, a bank is visible approaching the road from the right, and continuing on the other side. It actually travels on right down to Hurn Road and the river, and is a curious feature found marked on an 18th century map as the Hen Ditch, or Hen's Ditch. It is probably an ancient boundary, but survived as a parish boundary into the modern era.

Pursue the right-hand bank on its right-hand side as far as the summit of the pathway, then turn right, leaving Hen Ditch to ramble on towards Sopley.

At the top of the rise are the remains of some of the quarrying activity for sand and gravel – appearing here to have been on a commercial scale. On the left are the most extraordinary and beautiful views across the Avon Valley far below. Relish it while you can: one day that controversial but apparently much desired bypass may stampede through with all its ugliness, destruction and screaming assault on the ears.

Meanwhile, note the small mound at the crest – a mixture of sand, gravel and soil. You may be surprised to learn that this is all that is left of yet another barrow, and one from which the co-author, Mike Tizzard, one day spotted the remains of an embedded circular pot. It was upturned and the base was worn off, leaving just a ring of orange clay in the ground. On its later excavation by him and colleagues from the South Wessex Archaeological Association (SWAA) it turned out to be a Bronze Age cremation urn of a youth together with the remains of a small cup, which were transferred to Southampton University.

Continue on this path at the edge of the hill, enjoying the spectacular views: Town Common actually extends down the hillside and across the plain as far, roughly, as the first set of electricity lines.

Keep to either of the parallel hillside tracks and pause at the bench, from where your view extends as far as the Needles of the Isle of Wight, weather permitting. If exceptionally clear, the Needles lighthouse can be seen.

Take the right fork behind the bench; notice another almost imperceptible barrow on the right, hard up against the small path and just before it starts to descend. You will next be looking down on another part of the immense worked-out sand quarry, with a pool of water at its bottom, wherein newts teem. The path becomes railed, and you will pass a gap for cyclists to use, after which are the remains of another barrow, substantially eroded and truncated by quarrying. Continue on this undulating path, taking care with the numerous tree roots, for some distance, and keep a lookout for a large bowl-barrow close by your path on the right – unfortunately sprouting mature trees.

Rejoin the main track, proceeding left. The rails eventually finish, but keep walking a considerable distance, at first keeping close to the quarry ridge and then close to the crest of the hill where a myriad of tracks appear to confuse. You will reach another splendid viewpoint, easily identified by its triangulation pillar (keep your eyes open for the track leading to this on your left), from which you can see the town of Christchurch, with its dominating Priory Church spire, and Hengistbury Head beyond. When you can tear yourself away, rejoin the main path, retracing your steps right. Bear left at the path junction. A flagpole ahead will tell you if Christchurch Gun Club is operational: if there is a red flag, it is! Continue, bearing right.

View from the summit: towards Dudmoor. The common extends just under halfway to the lake. The line of our first railway is also visible: the service commenced in 1862 and ceased in 1935

Take the first path on the left and turn left at the top onto the track, passing the Roman Signal Station once more (on your right). Turn right again and proceed to a clearing. Insignificant as it appears to be, this was the site of another feature of our Cold War defences: for ten feet below you is a sealed-off bunker capable of holding four people in an emergency situation (note the telltale lumps of concrete in the ground) – another Royal Signals Corps legacy.

Take the hollowed-out path second left – undoubtedly, its sunken character indicates its considerable age – noting on the wider track you soon meet, the Gun Club to the left. Pass through the gate beyond it and continue straight over.

This delightful descent from the hill takes you past several old thatched cottages, constructed on the common by determined and opportunist 'potboilers' vividly recalled by Robert Starks, but here to stay, despite his fears.

Leave your walk at the Creed's Cross car park, where you commenced it, maybe a little wearily, but enriched by the variety and beauty of your ramble, which we hope you managed to, quite literally, keep track of.

Leaving Town Common by Marsh Lane

Coward's (Cowherd's) Marsh

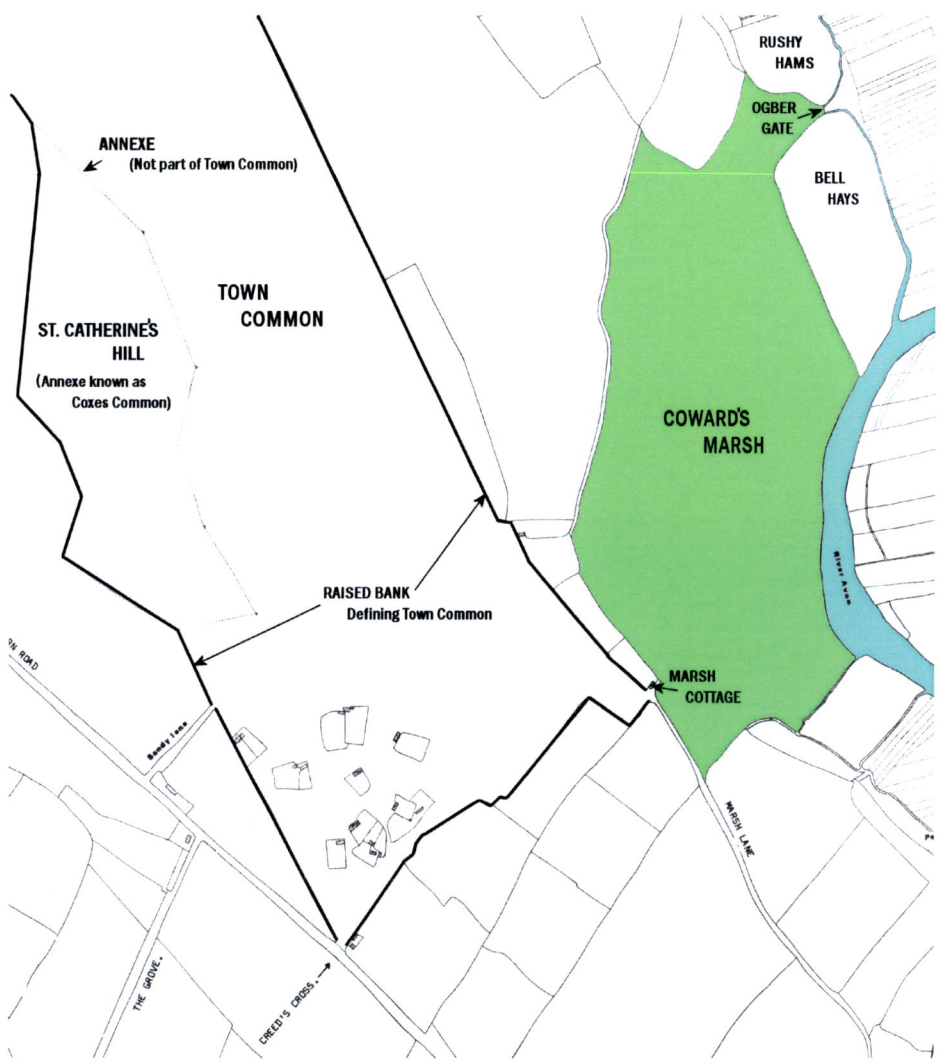

Note this boundary definition shows the 'grey area' of Coxes Common on Town Common (see above).
It is based on the tithe map

Its 69 acres of rich river meadow land and furze with extensive common rights ensures that no other Christchurch common has greater importance, an importance glimpsed in intriguing detail from the surviving minute books going back to 1752.

Doubtless originating in the Saxon era, its first recorded mention to survive is from 1575. John Farnell, a labourer, was leased half an acre by the corporation. He had to agree to build a single-roomed house (dimensions just 16 feet square, but with a small 'cote' at one end), at his own expense, and to take charge of the marsh and its ditches. No evidence exists of whether this tiny hut was ever constructed.

In 1614, the Lord of the Manor of Christchurch, Lord Arundel of Wardour, granted one and a half acres of waste to the Mayor and Burgesses to house a herdsman ('heards man') to keep the fences in repair and keep out stray animals. He had to impound the animals if they were not legitimately on the marsh, and prevent unlawful trespass. His rent was two fat geese each Christmas. This was the first Marsh House, and the lease locates it 'without the north gate of Knapp (otherwise Latch) Farm': it was therefore just outside the entrance gate to Coward's Marsh (see Walk for location of this gate).

A census was conducted of the town's inhabitants in 1601 in which 32 townspeople signed their consent to an order that commoners might put only two 'Rother' (cattle) beasts or one horse at the breach of the marsh', an early directive which holds sway still (but see the 'order' of 1632 quoted below). The breach was fixed as 21 May, and was celebrated with a Marsh Fair right up until the First World War, at which beer and buns were bought and distributed amongst the adults and the children (the town documents of October 1858 allow 'for beer and other things when we went to seak for Coward's Marsh'), a custom revived in 1954 at his own expense by Tom MacArdle, a prominent commoner.

The Marsh Fair c.1950s
Left to right: Tom McArdle; Charles Perry; Alfred Newman (steward); Arthur Starks (herdsman); woman unknown; Steve Coles of Latch Farm; Allen White (photographer and local historian, back to camera); Les Newman senior; Mr Hayball in foreground with back to camera; others unidentified

On 12 August, Lammas Day, Coward's Marsh was closed and the cattle driven into neighbouring Ogber. On 2 October, the day that the accounts were audited at the Marsh

House and stewards (quaintly entitled 'Mayors of Cowards Marsh' in some early entries in the accounts) and a herdsman appointed by the commoners, both marshes were thrown open for grazing. This provided a huge 138-acre field, for a fee, right through to Candlemas on 14 February the following year. The following is an account of the occasion from the reminiscences of Robert Starks (1845-1922):

When the day came for turning out the cattle onto the marsh it was called Mesh Fair and the men that went there was given a pint of ale and the children a bun. The boys used to run races for money or cakes, and the girls as well – it was a sort of half-holiday. I don't know if these things are still carried on.

That it was, at least periodically, is shown by the photograph on page 20, taken around the 1950s.

In addition to the grazing rights, commoners also had the right to cut furze (gorse; a right of estover), a valuable fuel and litter material. References occur to a resolution of the stewards and commoners made in 1718, the original of which appears to have been lost, that the poor may *'fetch it home at their backs'.* That this was another privilege prone to abuse is indicated by a resolution passed in 1826 to put a stop to the carting away of the furze by wheelbarrow. It was necessary to curtail this somewhat excessive exercise of this right: *'It is hereby agreed that no furze be carried away but as usual, viz. with a prong or fork on their backs.'* The early 19th century was a time of extreme rural destitution, so the situation might reflect the desperate straits the cottagers of the town were reduced to.

These annually elected stewards were responsible from 1752 for all matters relating to the management of the marsh. Whilst earlier records of their affairs do not survive, occasionally problems encountered would be raised at the Court Leet. In 1631 one Robert Dunman *'made a way by Coward's Marsh and Ogber and opened a gate there to the injury of the vill of Christchurch, wherefore he is ordered not to use that way for passage under the penalty of 10s.'* That was a substantial penalty to be risked for endangering the cattle in that way again.

The surviving records reveal much of interest about the affairs of the marsh, opening with the final payment of £14 spent on building Marsh House, or rebuilding it: a process repeated in 1836 (the accounts imply that all of the previous medieval building was taken down).

However, for the most part the money being spent was on improving access - many references occur to bridges being repaired or replaced, providing a dry route across particularly wet areas; weeds were cut, locks acquired for the gate, trenching, banking (once in 1775, for keeping the sheep out), hedging; rails and rubbing posts for the beasts; mending the cartway and the stile, paying for tar and twine, thatch for the Marsh House, leather and paper for the account books and so on.

The reference to hedging and ditching arises from the marsh being at the time enclosed by a bank and thorn hedge (as would, probably, all the other commons).

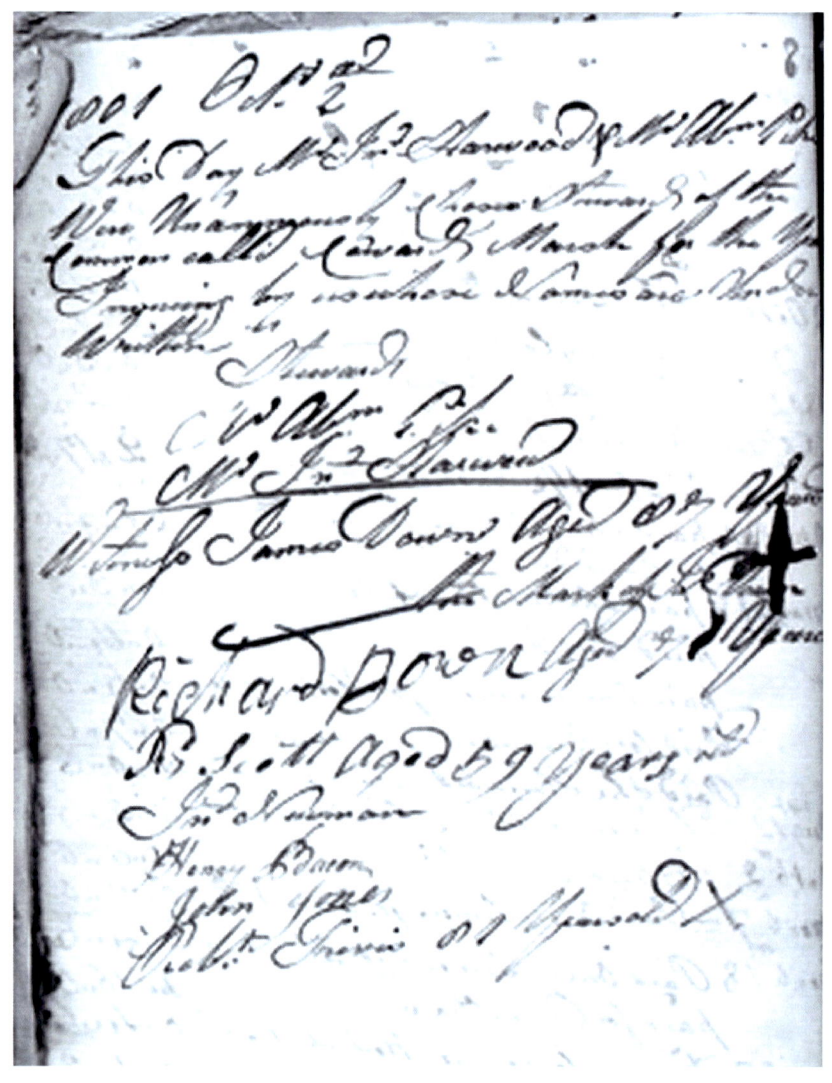

Extract from the Commoners' Accounts, with examples of signatures, 1801

From a chance reference to it, it would appear that such labour was recruited at that most excellent of labour exchanges: the pub, in this case the Country House, which stood in the middle of Bargates. Every year there was expenditure on beer, tobacco, biscuits and buns for the breach, money to the town crier to cry the opening of the marsh, and payments for the driving of the animals into or out of Ogber.

Account of Money Received at The Breech £ s d

	£	s	d
1796 May 2 Mr Fill Mr Newman 1 Horse	0	3	0
Recd Mr M Pike 2 Cows not paid	0	3	0
S Mr Rich Scott	0	3	0
S Mr James Seymour 2 Cows	0	3	0
S Mr John Harwood 1 Horse	0	3	0
S Mr Robt Banister 2 Colts	0	3	0
S Mr Henry Bacon 1 Horse	0	3	0
S Mr Pridout 1 Horse	0	3	0
S Mr W Holloway 1 Horse	0	3	0
Mr Robt Gale 1 Horse	0	3	0
S Mr J Newman 1 Horse	0	3	0
S Mr R Verge 1 Horse	0	3	0
S Mr J William 1 Horse a Colt	0	4	0
S Mr J Jones 1 Horse	0	3	0
S Mr Lemon 1 Cow	0	1	6
S Mr Morgan 1 Cow	0	1	6
S Mr P Jenkins 1 Horse	0	3	0
S Mr A Pike 1 Horse	0	3	0
S Mr Plate 1 Horse	0	3	0
S Mr Thos Bannister 1 Horse a Colt	0	2	6
S Mr J Aldridge 1 Horse	0	3	0
S Mr A Quartly 1 Horse	0	3	0
S Mr M Stocks 1 Horse	0	3	0
S Mr H Hart 1 Horse	0	3	0
S Mr R Tyzard 1 Horse	0	3	0
S Mr J Travers 1 Cow	0	1	6
S Mr B Aldridge 2 Cows	0	3	0
S Mr J Prince 2 Cows	0	3	0
S Mr Richd Bound 2 Cows	0	3	0
S Mr David Tyzard 1 Horse	0	3	0
S Mr C Davis 2 Cows	0	3	0
S Mr Thos Boodly 2 Horse Colts	0	3	0
Mr Molcham 1 Cow	0	1	6
Carried over	4	13	6

Page from the Coward's Marsh accounts, 1796

A very interesting feature of the accounts is the dialect and use of words otherwise quite obsolete. Especially intriguing are references, every year, to the payments for a man to kill 'the wants'. It gradually becomes clear, aided by recourse to the full OED, that this is a local word for 'mole'. Why this word occasionally becomes 'mould' must be for other reasons: an oft-repeated spelling error probably reflecting the pronunciation. James Durnford had this job for many years in these 18th century accounts.

Another mystery is the purchase of 'frith' from local farmers. This turned out to be brushwood, and it is likely it was being used to make fences with to divide up the marsh and therefore the cattle, or to encircle it in its entirety.

A blank page occurs in the accounts in 1779, except for the remark: '*What money wasted in the year 1779 I cannot find*'!

So much for expenditure: the income was obtained from fees paid at the Marsh Fair to admit the animals. The order of 1633 referred to above quoted a fee of 2½d quarterly (10d a year); the surviving accounts quote a modest 1s 6d for a horse and 9d for a cow, the fee was double by 1813 and not apparently increased again until after World War One (5s and 2s 6d respectively). By 1953 a horse cost 10s for a season's grazing and a cow half that amount, and in 1983 each cow or horse would cost the owner £20. Somehow, the books always seemed to balance and stay in the black despite the caustic comment made in 1779. It is greatly interesting to note that it would appear from a study of the names that the horse-owners were the gentry, and the cows belonged to the humbler classes.

Some of the users of Coward's Marsh are renowned for other reasons in the town's history: John Streeter, for instance, the notorious smuggler, kept a horse there in 1775 and 1778; Robert Cox, who brought the manufacture of fusee chains to the town, kept his horse there from 1780. Dr Thomas Jeans, another noted inhabitant, paid over his three shillings for his horse in 1793: one of the shillings was bad! A large proportion of the less fortunate members of society signed their names with a cross, or in a very ill-practised hand. Occasionally, very valuable information about individuals may be gleaned: John West is described as a glover in 1767, William Hookey a cooper and a Mr Aldridge a baker (both 1770) - all of use to social and family historians.

In 1632 a list was drawn up by the corporation: '*by an order by the Jurie at a Lawdaye . . . what beasts several householders shall keep*', and promptly listed the users of the marsh and their entitlement of two, three or four beasts! On what basis this order was arrived at is a mystery, but the impression is given of people being classified by some criteria – wealth and power, most likely, but it could relate to the amount of land they held to use for their animals when the commons were closed or overcrowded.

The appointment of the herdsman was an important decision, as he had to be on site to attend to all day-to-day matters concerning the marsh. In 1791 the gloriously named

Onesimus (or even Onesiphorus) Summers was engaged, and remained in the post for the incredible length of time of 45 years, his name abbreviated to Oney. Many entries in the ledger concern his duties, including the cutting of the furze, which was then sold - if not spirited away: a memorandum carefully entered in 1834 by Hiram Hiscock tells the sad tale of 600 faggots cut, *'out of which there was but 340 sold, 260 lost or stolen'*. It appears that the proceeds were meant to have been distributed to the town's poor folk.

The herdsman's principal duty was, of course, to the animals and their owners, being required to check the animals regularly, find and advise the owners of anything amiss with them, make sure no animals came in at the gate which did not belong to Old Borough householders, keep the stewards informed of any 'depredations', and keep his Marsh House in repair. Certainly, ascertaining who was a legitimate commoner became an increasingly difficult task, so much so that the stewards had to threaten legal action against some impostors by the mid-19th century. Things were to get even worse in this respect: so bad that the stewards resolved in 1891 to refuse to admit any cattle which the owner could not prove he had owned for a month. People were plainly selling their commonable rights to those not entitled to use the marsh themselves.

Eventually, the herdsman's role was further defined, to include keeping out stallions or bulls to prevent them fraternising with the female animals; keeping the ditches clear, stopping people shooting wildfowl without authority; and repairing the banks, ditches and fences. Illicit shooting of wildfowl and game was a routine problem on the marsh, though never as contentious as it became in neighbouring Ogber. In later periods the stewards did grant shooting rights for a fee.

As this early employment contract was actually formulated in 1836 after the departure of Oney, we may safely assume that the house maintenance rule was introduced because of the dilapidation of Marsh House, which had to be pulled down and entirely rebuilt that year, though still in cob and thatch, by Charles Davis, at a cost of £18 17s.

As the years go on, commoning practices plainly change with the times and new problems arise: in 1869, for instance, guano (decomposed bat dung) was bought for the first time, carried from Lymington. It would have been used to feed the grass. Costing then over £5, it was not cheap, but must have been useful as the following year double was spent on 'artificial manure'. Presumably the ton of bone dust spread on the ground the previous year had been insufficiently effective. The First World War produced such a dire food shortage that cattle were not permitted to be fed grain, and for once the limitation on the numbers of animals allowed on the marsh was lifted. The restriction was again lifted in 1932, as so few cattle were by that time being kept by the householders of the Old Borough, unsurprisingly. By 1983 the maximum permitted number per commoner was raised to twelve cows or six horses, reflecting the sharp decline in individual ownership of grazing animals by the late 20th century.

The greatest challenge faced by the commoners was the Regulation issue of the early 1920s, which met with a furious protest and resolutions and petitions drafted to counter the perceived threat. This scheme, proposed by the Rural District Council, was for control to be invested in that body. The commoners objected to Coward's Marsh being included in the scheme, which was principally devised for Town Common. The commoners won the day. They were not immediately so successful in a serious dispute with the Malmesbury Estate in 1982, when they were taken to court by Lord Malmesbury over the estate's claim that virtually all those claiming to have rights in the marsh had not registered their claim under the 1965 Commons Registration Act and had as a result lost their common rights. The commoners argued that the marsh was not manorial waste of the Manor of the Borough, not even being within the boundaries of that manor, and was not therefore the property of the Malmesbury Estate but of the inhabitants of the Old Borough. The Marsh Fair was revived at this time (see illustration) to raise funds to finance the costly legal action. Eventually, a settlement was reached whereby the estate gave up all its claimed rights - it was bought off.

Front page of the programme for the revived Marsh Fair, 1981

However, the commoners were out of pocket, and their fair programme of 1981 plaintively appeals: *'During the last two decades the number of active commoners has declined, mainly because the vast majority of the inhabitants of the Old Borough of Christchurch do not know of the facilities available to them by right. We must recruit more members . . .'*

Today, the marsh's ownership has been vested in the Christchurch Commoners' Association, as a result of a successful Heritage Lottery bid in 1998. The price for ten months' of pasturage is currently £30 for a horse and half that for a cow.

Walk

The commoners permit freedom to roam: please take all caution with dogs kept on the lead as there are cattle and horses as well as wildfowl and small animals to have consideration for. Take care in the winter as conditions are very muddy – you are entering onto a river meadow, after all!

The entrance to Coward's Marsh is obtained from the car park anciently known as Creed's Cross, off Fairmile, marked 'Dudmoor', on the right-hand side of Fairmile as you proceed from the town. Take the metalled Marsh Lane roadway from that point. Take care of periodic road traffic.

Keep on the road, noting on the left a rare section of cob wall surviving at the end of a cottage on your left, next to a brick entrance archway. This is an ancient and cheap DIY method of cottage construction from centuries past: mixing clay or mud, horse or cow manure with straw to form a thick and sticky mix which could be built up layer by layer to form a structure.

Pass the road to Dudmoor Farm on the left, at which point bear right and soon afterwards a wide break in the vegetation reveals the entrance to Coward's Marsh on the same side. Turn into this entrance and admire the recently restored Marsh House (illustrated), described above. It is still occupied by the herdsman.

Marsh House

Opposite is a pathway running alongside animal pens, leading to a stile, from which access to the marsh is obtained. After the stile, turn left and head for the main pathway over the marsh and cross the bridge over the cut drainage ditch. You will be entering onto what has become, since the Second World War, one of the remaining 5% of unimproved meadows, and the birds, insects and flowers abundant in the warmer seasons will delight naturalists and those with a love of the countryside alike. We devised this walk in May, while bluebells abounded in the shadier glades, and flag iris thrived in the boggier conditions, noting also white campion and celandine: many more will be seen by the more discerning (see Felicity Woodhead's *The Flora of Christchurch*, for a meticulously detailed list of flowers to be found throughout the year).

Such natural charm and idyllic rarity are all the more precious for long having been coveted for a proposed bypass. What a price to pay and what precious treasures to be lost forever should that ever materialise.

Cattle depastured on the marsh; the trees leading to Ogber Gate behind them, shown on page 29

Ogber Gate

You will now need to make your way to Ogber Gate (though you may detour to the River Avon for further scenic and wildlife interest): follow the path on the right, heading for the clumps of trees in the distance, and those on the right in particular. A ditch leading through the trees on your right is also leading to the same destination. This is what you need to look out for.

This gate occupies a narrow opening between the two commons; the enclosures either side are not part of either. Cross over the gate and continue, if wished, the walk onto Ogber, described on page 32.

Ogber

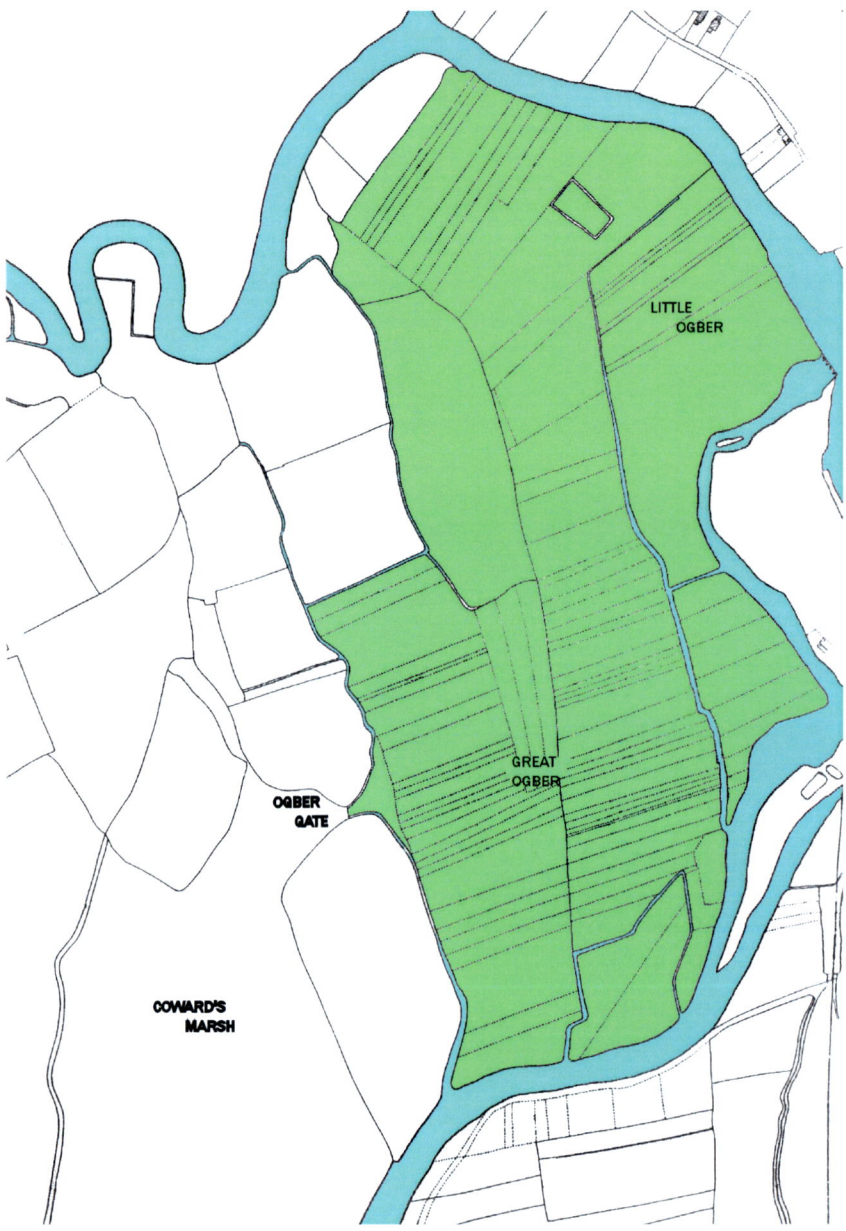

Ogber, based on the tithe map

Its name derived from 'Okebere', or oak wood, this area of 66 acres of meadow lies contingent with Coward's Marsh and is in every other respect closely associated with it. As with its neighbour, its exact ownership and manorial history appear to be somewhat confused, but it is recorded as being within the Manor of Hurn in an 1811 perambulation of that manor.

It is a free pasture for the inhabitants of the Old Borough, and open to them from Lammas Day, 12 August, notice of which would be shouted about the streets of the town by the crier. On this day the stewards, herdsman and householders would all meet in Ogber for the great drive of the beasts out of Coward's Marsh, through Ogber Gate which was opened between them, and all cattle not legitimately permitted on Ogber would be promptly impounded and only released on payment of a fee. At the closure of both marshes on Candlemas (14 February), the cattle would be taken up to Town Common for grazing until the breach of Coward's Marsh on 21 May. This type of common right was known as the 'aftermath', i.e. the right to graze after the hay had been cut. Grazing and hay-cutting rights would revert to the owners during the closed season until Lammas came round again. The landowners also had strips like the commoners did. Both pastures were open from 2 October at the annual Coward's Marsh audit.

An early reference to this practice is contained in the town documents: *'October 1658. When we went to drove Ogber and the field, 1s 8d.'*

The 1844 Tithe Map (on page 30) shows how Ogber was intensively cultivated even at that date by the medieval strip system.

Ogber was regulated by the stewards and herdsman of Coward's Marsh in all respects, except being a free common it did not require the same careful accounting. Being the lesser common in various respects, it would appear to have been somewhat neglected, suffering from clogged watercourses and overgrown tracks by the later 19th century. It was similarly subjected to impassioned legal disputes about its ownership and rights, exacerbated in particular in the 19th century by that most determined sportsman and litigant, Grantley Berkeley, of Winkton House just across the Avon. A flurry of court actions followed the grant to him of all shooting rights by the Earl of Malmesbury, during which various commoners were charged with trespassing in pursuit of game. 35 commoners signed a petition in 1862 (Lord Malmesbury bought the Manor of Borough in 1863, recorded Herbert Druitt) and presented it to Lord Malmesbury, which whilst acknowledging his ownership of most of the land, claimed they had always been permitted to shoot there by his predecessors without challenge. Grantley Berkeley insisted that *'all the feather and fur in Ogber belong to him by permission of the Earl of Malmesbury'*, and the noble earl loftily advised the commoners that he was unable to withdraw the shooting rights once granted. The following year Lord Malmesbury increased the general atmosphere of hostility by issuing shooting tickets for the adjacent Coward's Marsh; he must have been deeply unpopular with the commoners, who were by and large killing game to eat and not for the sport alone.

Despite these claims, it would appear that land in Ogber passed with freehold premises in the town: an advert in *The Salisbury Journal* on 15 July 1822, sought a purchaser for a *'neat and convenient Dwelling-House, lately erected . . . situated at Stanpit'* which came complete with land at both Ogber and another meadow nearby known as Podney. An earlier entry, on 2

February 1790, related to a freehold dwelling house in South Bockhampton, which came with an acre of meadow in Ogber *'near Sopley Mark'* (ie, at the north-western edge). This meadow was occupied by one Joseph Vick. This interestingly demonstrates that ownership of the Ogber strips was widely spread in the parish, not confined to the Old Borough inhabitants, and could also be sold despite having an existing user, who, presumably, had rights to continue to utilise the strip.

Walk

From Ogber Gate, again keeping dogs on a lead and taking care on very wet ground, wander through the meadow towards the houses of Stoney Lane, Winkton, in the far distance.

Once again, enjoy the buttercups, kingcups, ragged robin and other flora, the birds, including lapwings, and, in the summertime, a abundance of butterflies.

This common was once clearly demarcated into narrow strips, and when conditions are right and you are particularly perceptive, you may note traces of them still lingering on.

Eventually, you will reach a distinct bank and watery, overgrown ditch, the demarcation between Great Ogber behind you, and Little Ogber ahead. Walk no further at this point.

There were, and may be still, depressions at the north end ('Enderditch') which are the remains of a curious enterprise: sand diggings for the glass industry. This practice was apparently commenced about 1950 by a Mr Maidment of Dudmoor, and arose from the fine quality of the sand. Return to Ogber Gate and exit via Coward's Marsh as above.

Returning towards the town on foot or by car, you will pass the following features:

The Old Borough bound stone which still stands along Fairmile Road between Knapp Mill Avenue and Rimbury Way is an ancient marker for a change in direction of the Old Borough boundary (long since changed and enlarged). The boundary here more or less enclosed and marked the extent of Portfield. The setting of the old stone is today somewhat overshadowed by street furniture and is not quite in its original position.

One side of the stone is angled; this denotes the change in direction of the boundary parameter. To the west it ran to a small group of Bronze Age barrows (long gone) both sides of Barrack Road, near to the barrack entrance, the two closest to it being known as Porpoise Hill (in medieval times referred to as 'the mound').

To the east from the bound stone the boundary ran to a water channel that once fed one of Christchurch's lost mills above Knapp on the east bank of the Avon, the marker point being commonly known as the 'Alder Bush'. The bush, channel and mill have long gone.

The Old Borough boundary is very ancient and quite likely dates from Saxon times. It is also likely, as it was on the west, that the stone originally marked a spot where a barrow once stood. There are a number of barrows in the vicinity and they were often used as boundary markers.

There is an entry in the borough accounts for a payment for a bound stone in the 17th century but whether this is the same stone is uncertain.

The stone itself is rather curious. About ten years ago (c.1997) it was unceremoniously dug up and moved, owing to road widening. This gave co-author Mike Tizzard the opportunity to examine it in some detail before it was re-interred.

From the photo, the top, as would be expected, looks quite weathered but the lower part is not, having a clean break, and making the stone about three feet long. Originally, the stone was clearly much longer, perhaps six feet or more, but subsequently it has been broken and repaired with a number of iron cleats, one of which still survived set into the stone and there are also clear marks of several others.

The bound stone, showing the iron cleat top right

A stone of such a length was obviously meant as a permanent, immovable marker but then future service trenches and road widening were never taken into account. Hopefully, the broken base is still *in situ* in its original position.

A few years later the stone was again pulled up, not by the council this time, but by some local youths testing their strength. The remaining iron cleat, however, had gone!

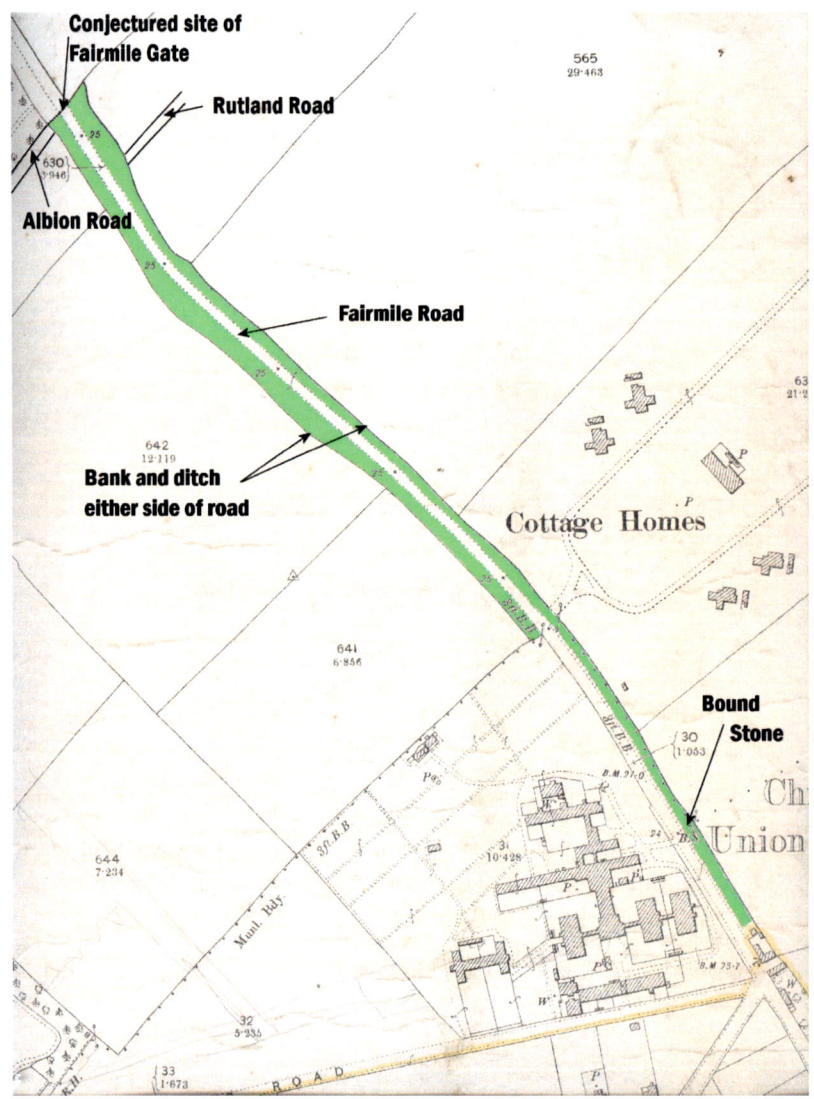

Conjectured site of Fairmile Gate

Rutland Road

565
29·463

Albion Road

630
?·946

25

Fairmile Road

642
12·119

Bank and ditch either side of road

63
21·2

Cottage Homes

641
6·856

Bound Stone

30
1·053

B.M.91·0.

Ch·

Union

644
7·234

30.R.B

31
10·428

24

B.M 73·1

32
5·235

Mun. Bdy.

W·C·

33
1·673

R · O · A · D

Fairmile Map, based on 1899 OS showing the features mentioned

Just south of the bound stone, more or less where the fire station now stands, was the end of the sprawl of mud cottages that ran up from the town both sides of Fairmile Road. From this point you may notice the grass verges becoming wider either side of the main road (more noticeable in the days before the road was widened).

These wide verges were described by Herbert Druitt (*The Book of Bournemouth*) as 'wayside manor-commons' and were not part of the highway and should be preserved as such. He quotes the 'List of the Commoning' made by the then steward, the solicitor, Henry Rowden, in 1825, pertaining to the former monastic property adjacent to the bound stone, Latch Farm, where there was mention of an area of 6a 2r 34p (acres, rods and perches), 'Part of Fairmile Road'.

The verges were once bounded on the outside by a ditch and a hedge-topped bank in front of the fields behind. The hedges have long gone and the ditches filled; the banks, however, still survive in places and where they have not, the course can be traced by property front boundaries in which some have very characteristic crooked oak trees growing along them. These trees have a kink at their base that is indicative of growing out of a bank.

The bank and impression of its ditch lining Fairmile

The best example is a short section running up as far as Rutland Road which is still topped by such oaks. This section was once much longer, running north beyond Rutland Road, and had a row of elm trees growing along it which have succumbed to the dreaded elm disease. The bank and trees were unfortunately destroyed when landscaping the area in front of the estate there, just a few years ago. This section of bank (its course still just visible) ran off at a slight angle away from the road (see map, page 34) and abruptly ended at a boundary at right angles to Fairmile Road, opposite Albion Road.

It is probable that Fairmile Gate was sited at this point so it could close off Fairmile Road from the heath beyond, thus keeping cattle from entering, or even leaving. There are no known records to pinpoint the exact location of this gate, but many refer to its existence. The Old Corporation looked after Fairmile Gate along with the banks, hedges and ditches. There are many entries about them in the borough accounts, for they were in constant need of repair. Such entries go back to the early 16th century.

Unfortunately, earlier accounts are now lost.

Fairmile Gate's conjectured site across Fairmile Road

The gate and banks would have formed long, enclosed, grazing strips and would almost certainly have been used by travellers, fairgoers and their animals after a long journey. It's therefore quite conceivable that impromptu fairs and trading went on prior to the two main fairs in the town, which were of huge economic importance to Christchurch; this trading is the most likely explanation of the name Fairmile (at the top of Bargates there is an area called Fairfield); the earlier medieval name for Fairmile Road was Port Lane.

Portfield

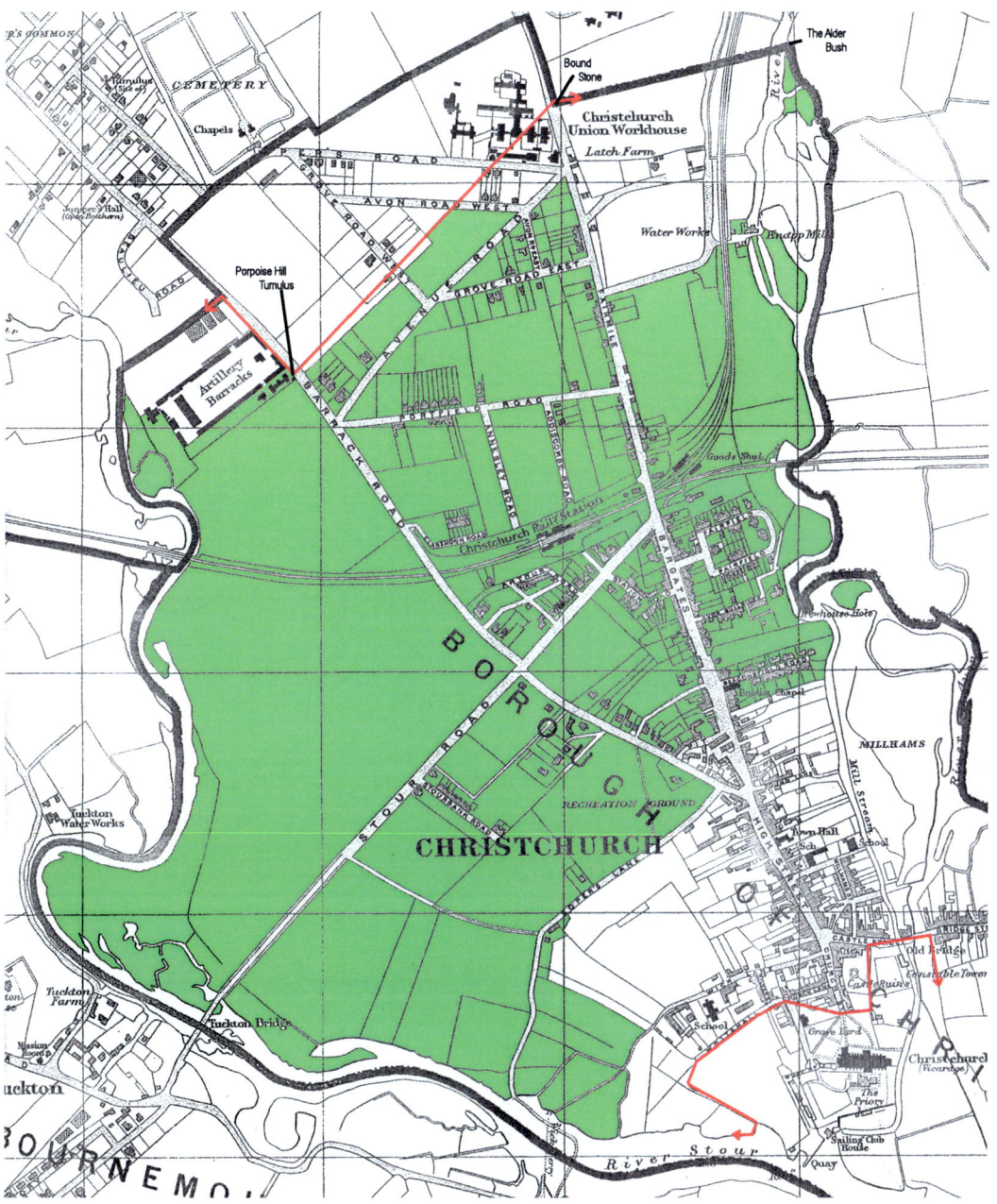

Bright's map of Bournemouth 1904, superimposed with the extent of and boundary of Portfield as recorded by the tithe map. Note it includes land east of Sopers Lane. No earlier sources exist for the boundary of Portfield, which may well have once extended further up the side of the Lane and further northwards. The next but one land portion above that shown east of Sopers Lane is Dean's Close, an unlawful enclosure – see Quomps. The small sections at the top right are Knapp Farm, one of the most ancient mills in this town of rivers. The red line is part of the Old Borough boundary

The last of the common lands for the inhabitants of the Old Borough is, at around 280 acres (251 acres, 1 rod and 26 perches is precisely given in an 1867 directory), the largest, stretching from Sopers Lane right up to Jumpers Common, and is different from the other commons in being largely arable land (but 20 acres were meadow), although it was probably all grassland in earlier times. A fertile strip of river meadows alongside the Stour is distinguished within Portfield as 'Marshfield' and provided valuable pasture. The division between the two parts was called Marsh Ditch, and now passes between Twynham School and its playing fields in the form of a path, as depicted in the walk.

The map on page 37, following the tithe map of 1844, indicates a greater extent to Portfield east of Sopers Lane than does the 1878 Enclosure Award, and suggests extensive private enclosures on that side. It also implies that centuries ago, Portfield could have extended beyond the boundaries shown to a lesser or greater degree. By 1878, when the land was enclosed, both the Youth Centre and Fairfield were excluded from Portfield, and many gardens in Bargates.

No charter exists to grant the rights attached to Portfield, which were all customary. These rights were those of pasturage, which was free to qualifying inhabitants from Lammas in August, through to Candlemas in February. Many properties in the town had deeds which included small strips of land in Portfield. An example, from *The Salisbury Journal* of 21 August 1775, is for a dwelling house in Bolt's Lane (the former name of Pound Lane) in the borough, with not only five and a half acres of mainly arable land in West Marsh, but two acres in Portfield, freehold but subject to a quit-rent.

 A Court Leet for the Manor of the Borough in 1632 decreed that: '*None shall depasture any other sheep in the Ersh in the Common Fields under the Penalty for every offence 10s and licence is given to any person to tye Asses or Horses upon their land after the first day of August in the Fields aforesaid at their pleasure*'.

The word ersh is an ancient one for stubble, suggesting the common fields referred to must have been Portfield. The first day in August was, of course, Lammas Day. The common rights were known as 'in shack', which strange description meant that beasts could wander at large on the stubble when the land was fallow.

Originally, the ownership of Portfield was divided between the Lord of the Manor of the Borough and the Priory's Manor of Christchurch-Twyneham, which around the year 1300 carved up its estate amongst tenants. The inhabitants cultivated the plots in typical medieval strip field patterns. A survey of the parish published in 1801 (*The Hampshire Repository*) indicated that the main crops were wheat and barley, but turnips were also grown and there would have been a system of crop rotation which had regular periods of fallow, or no crops grown.

Old documents concerning leases of land in Portfield contain interesting information about lost features, particularly of land *'near the barrows'*, which were Bronze Age round barrows situated near to the 18th century barracks each side of Barrack Road and lost by the middle of the following century. They had been used as the markers at that point for the boundary of the Old Borough. The Butts are also mentioned: archery practice ground on the site of the present flowerbeds adjacent to the road on the town recreation ground. The site extends under the widened Barrack Road.

Local people valued their common rights highly, enabling them as they did to support their households by growing crops or pasturing cattle. This is amply demonstrated by a riot (as it was described) which took place one year, after the annual Mayor-making, at which a certain amount of Dutch courage was imbibed along with the beer freely handed out to the populace on these occasions. The immediate cause of the violent expression of their grievance was the construction of a house by a prominent businessman and burgess, John Edward Holloway. In 1847 he received permission from the Mary Magdalen Hospital charity for a lease to build a house on the site of their medieval 'lazar (leper) house' on the edge of the town, within Portfield. This was not the first such occasion, an earlier enclosure to erect a building had not been challenged because of the difficulties in proving anyone's rights had been thereby damaged. This earlier building was probably the present youth centre, The Lighthouse, on the recreation ground.

On this occasion, a considerable number (about 100) of local people decided to take direct action by breaking down all illegal enclosures in Portfield. Shouting that *'they would have their rights'*, and *'Portfield belongs to the poor'*, their campaigners started with Dean's Close, at the bottom of Sopers Lane (thus indicating that this was also considered to be part of Portfield – and it was where the gate into Quomps was sited), then they proceeded to Stocker's Mead where they dismantled a gate and trampled down further fences (probably Dashwin's Mead), more offending enclosures in Bargates (including, we suspect, Collin's Close), then on to the chief offender's newly-built house, Fairlight (at the corner of the present Magdalen Lane, then non-existent). Mr Holloway endeavoured to protect his fences by sitting on them but they were destroyed from under him. He told the crowd that the Corporation had permitted him to enclose the land, which certainly did nothing to enhance the crowd's appreciation of the conduct of the mayor and burgesses, who were plainly eroding their ancient rights. The resultant court case made great play of the fact that three of the four defendants were not inhabitant householders and the one that was had no cattle. That these common rights were held very dear to the poor people of the town was again amply demonstrated.

In earlier ages, other complaints survive about encroachments: powerful and greedy principal inhabitants had a habit of fencing off, or enclosing, parts of Portfield for themselves. On the other hand, documents survive which show that people not entitled to put their cattle on the land did so – possibly inadvertently; a man from Hurn and another from Iver (Iford) were fined 4d and 6d respectively in 1639 for this misdemeanour. The government of the day was able to override the rights in Portfield when the Barracks were constructed at the end of the 18th century, as a twin assault against the threat of a Napoleonic invasion, and to counter the rife smuggling trade.

For these reasons, the first attempt in 1855 to enclose Portfield so that it could be built on was so strongly resisted that it failed. The second attempt succeeded in 1878, when an Act of Parliament was passed which abolished the common rights in Portfield but in lieu of these granted to all the inhabitants ten acres for recreation and exercise, which is how we got the Barrack Road 'rec'. The rest of Portfield was laid out with new roads created by the act - Stour Road, Portfield Road, Jumpers Road and others, and the abolition of many ancient tracks and paths. The accompanying map to the Enclosure Award is the only known record of these lost 'green' lanes and has been reproduced on page 41, with the new roads deleted. The single most important aspect of this map is how so many of these lanes centred on the medieval leper hospital of St Mary Magdalen, indicating a hugely important institution which may have originated soon after the Conquest. Other features to note are the many lanes leading onto Coward's Marsh, and others to other commons such as Stocker's Mead.

Of interest, long before the enclosure road of Stour Road was constructed, and Tuckton Bridge over the Stour at the end of it with its tollbridge, there was a way known as Tuckton Road, leading down to the river, with a counterpart on the opposite bank – undoubtedly an early crossing point, possibly a ford.

In this area, yet another unlawful enclosure was bitterly contested: in 1657 the parcel of land (see map, page 59) called Tufton's Corner, also known as Tuckton Corner, was taken out of 'Cowslip Mead'. The Stevens family members were extremely powerful inhabitants of the town, being mercers and property owners, and spawning generations of successive mayors. This did not make them scrupulous. Thomas Stevens grabbed Tufton's Corner, kept it enclosed for himself, and refused to open it on Lammas Day. We wonder what made these people think they could ride roughshod over the rights of the inhabitants which went back 'tyme out of mind'. In this case the Corporation acted, and in a form of trial of the rights and title of Tufton's Corner, a majority 'subscribed' and the others did 'denyeth' a contribution to the costs of the legal action.

Some of the recreation ground was lost when a strip was taken to widen the road in 1960, but that is virtually the only legally permissible reason for taking what is called enclosure award land. This designation meant the ground was automatically eligible for registration as a village green, which was effected by Mr D Hewitt of this town. The protection afforded by village green status was successfully utilised when the recreation ground was being unlawfully used for circuses and car parking in the 1990s.

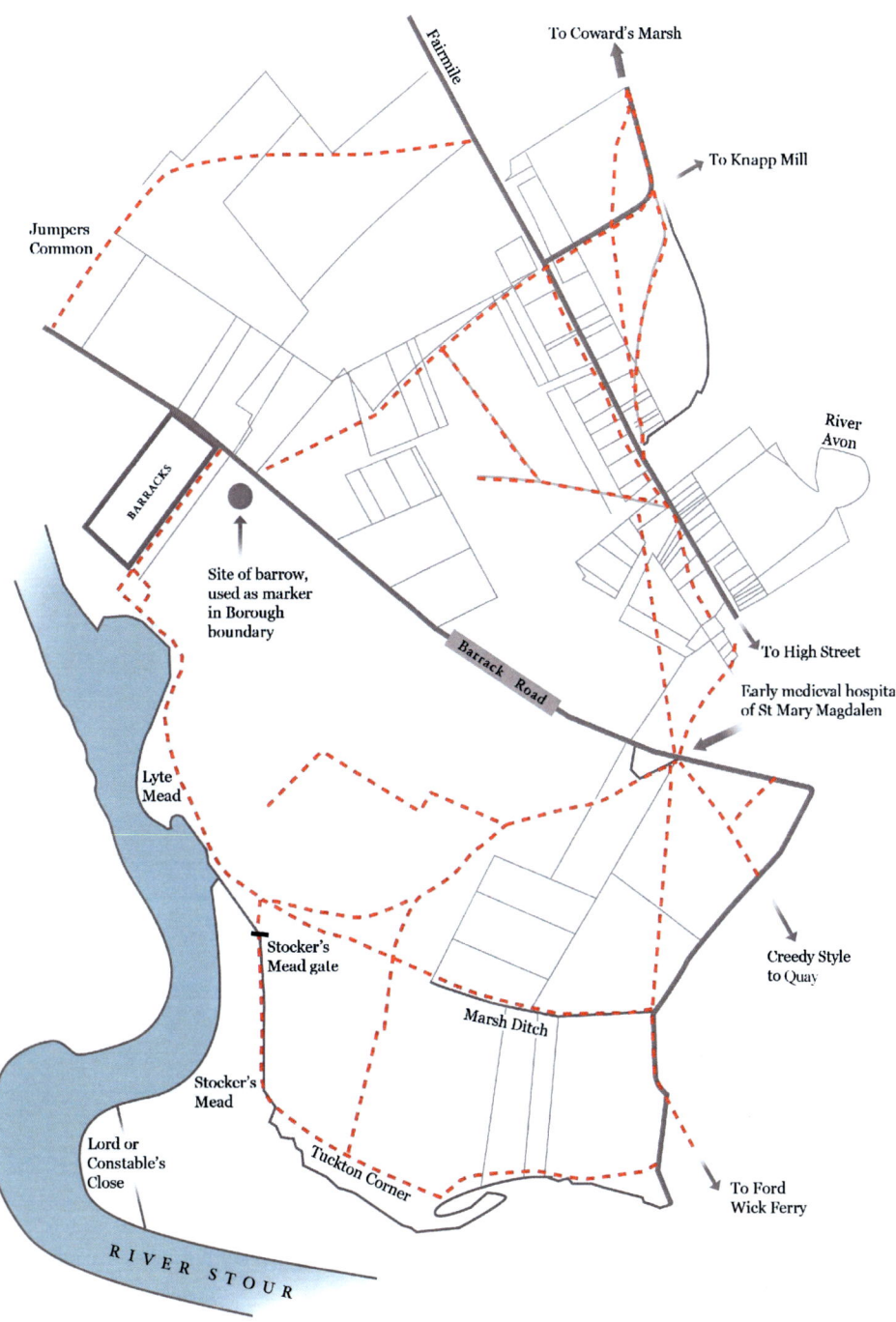

To Coward's Marsh

Fairmile

To Knapp Mill

Jumpers Common

River Avon

BARRACKS

Site of barrow, used as marker in Borough boundary

Barrack Road

To High Street

Early medieval hospital of St Mary Magdalen

Lyte Mead

Creedy Style to Quay

Stocker's Mead gate

Marsh Ditch

Stocker's Mead

Lord or Constable's Close

Tuckton Corner

To Ford Wick Ferry

RIVER STOUR

The original lanes and paths of Christchurch, created from 1878 Enclosure Award map
(shown by the red dotted lines)

The award also provided for a 15-acre stint (regulated pasture) ground at the former Tuckton Corner, permitting 129 (and a half!) sheep stints or rights of pasture. Each person entitled to do so could admit one sheep per stint, or one horse or cow per eight stints. This land is also now lost to housing (Willow Way).

The award occasionally defies all comprehension: the pathways alongside both sides of Sopers Lane were vested in the parishioners for the same purpose as the recreation ground: recreation and exercise. One wonders whether it would be lawful to play football on these pavements!

Walk

Not much is left of the original Portfield. You can still use the ancient Marsh Ditch, accessed either by the private road off Stour Road, South View Road, or from Sopers Lane to the left of the school. Much of the former Marshfield still floods in wet periods, a reminder of its apt original name. The field would have been divided, as most of Portfield was, into long and narrow strips for individual use, running north to south between the ditch and the river.

The Lighthouse Youth Club, on Barrack Road, is an early encroachment onto Portfield, it appears, dating from 1832. It has had a chequered history, from 'Emberley's timber yard' to the coal business of John Cooper Bemister, to Mrs Cox's photographic portrait studio; then the home of Ebenezer Barnard; a post-war Unemployment Benefit Office; a long period as the sports pavilion for the recreation ground clubs, and in more recent years the ignominious use as an amusement centre (during which use it lost its interior fittings). It has been splendidly refurbished in 2005/6 as a youth centre, and once again enhances the town. It was said by those who had once worked in it to be haunted by an invisible but noisy and active presence.

Pathway along the site of the Marsh Ditch

You may also visit the recreation ground. It was once recalled as growing a fine crop of hay. The central avenue is one of the lanes which survived the 1878 enclosure (and links to another, the Creedy Path running through Druitt Gardens), and it was a mayor living in Magdalen Lane, John Green, a High

Street chemist, who donated the avenue of trees at the end of his mayoral year in 1895. At the end of Magdalen Lane was the last remaining patch (as far as we are aware) of Portfield: a field of bramble and footpaths, with horses grazing the central grassy areas. Co-author Sue Newman clearly remembers that from living in the lane at the time that this remnant disappeared for housing in 1985. A local resident used to common her horse on this patch, and would urge her to make sure she also used her entitlement as a resident of the Old Borough! She was absolutely right, and a cow should have appeared on the field forthwith. The problems would have come in February when it would have to be relocated to her back garden.

Barrack Road recreation ground and ancient tree-lined path.
One of those preceding the 1878 Enclosure Award

The New Zealand flowerbeds at the corner of the top end of Sopers Lane have their own explanatory plaque.

At the junction of Sopers Lane and Barrack Road, before the A35 was widened so the spot is now under the extended carriageway, stood the wrought-iron archway entrance, with gas lamp atop, and a pair of stone lions. All this and the railings surrounding the ground were removed for the contentious iron reclamation during the Second World War.

At the top end of Magdalen Lane, at the junction with Barrack Road, and continuing under the tarmac of the widened east carriageway, was a very ancient institution known as the Mary Magdalen Hospital - a charity still in existence. It earliest deeds date right back to 1317, but it may in fact have been a Norman institution, as was the castle, the Priory, and the bargate.

The hospital owned a farm: the remnant of this is Castle Ironmongers in Bargates, which used to boast a huge barn alongside and there were also associated cottages running down what is now Magdalen Lane. Herbert Druitt, our indefatigable antiquarian hero, dug up 12th century (Early English) carved pieces in the grounds of the building you see at the top of the lane – known as Vancouver House (and the site of John Edward Holloway's 1847 encroachment, Fairlight). These carved stones are undoubtedly from the Leper Hospital, as it was, and enabled the site of No.1 Magdalen Lane, to enter the Dorset County Sites and Monuments Record and thus become archaeologically recognised and protected. This was most useful when an application was made to demolish the graceful late Victorian building on the site, Shortwood House. The carved pieces found by Herbert Druitt may well have been from the hospital chapel.

These Magdalen leper houses were sited outside the walls or boundaries of the town, and provided for those people afflicted by anything thought to be unpleasantly contagious. The buildings of the hospital seem to have disappeared sometime in the 17th century.

Another remnant of old Portfield remains by the Barracks. After its conversion to the Bailey Retail Park, a public footpath was created between the former guardhouse and the new Bailey Bridge Hotel. This meanders down towards the river, then curves right to what was once the garden behind the Officers' Mess (now apartments). These few acres border the Stour, and are a designated open space. One May morning in the rain, botanist Felicity Woodhead kindly assessed the meadow: some 140 different plant species were counted, and, later, insects such as the mayfly indicated a very rich and rare nature habitat, well worth a visit, and this open space may also be accessed from Dragoon Way alongside the guardhouse, now a hairdresser's salon.

Millhams

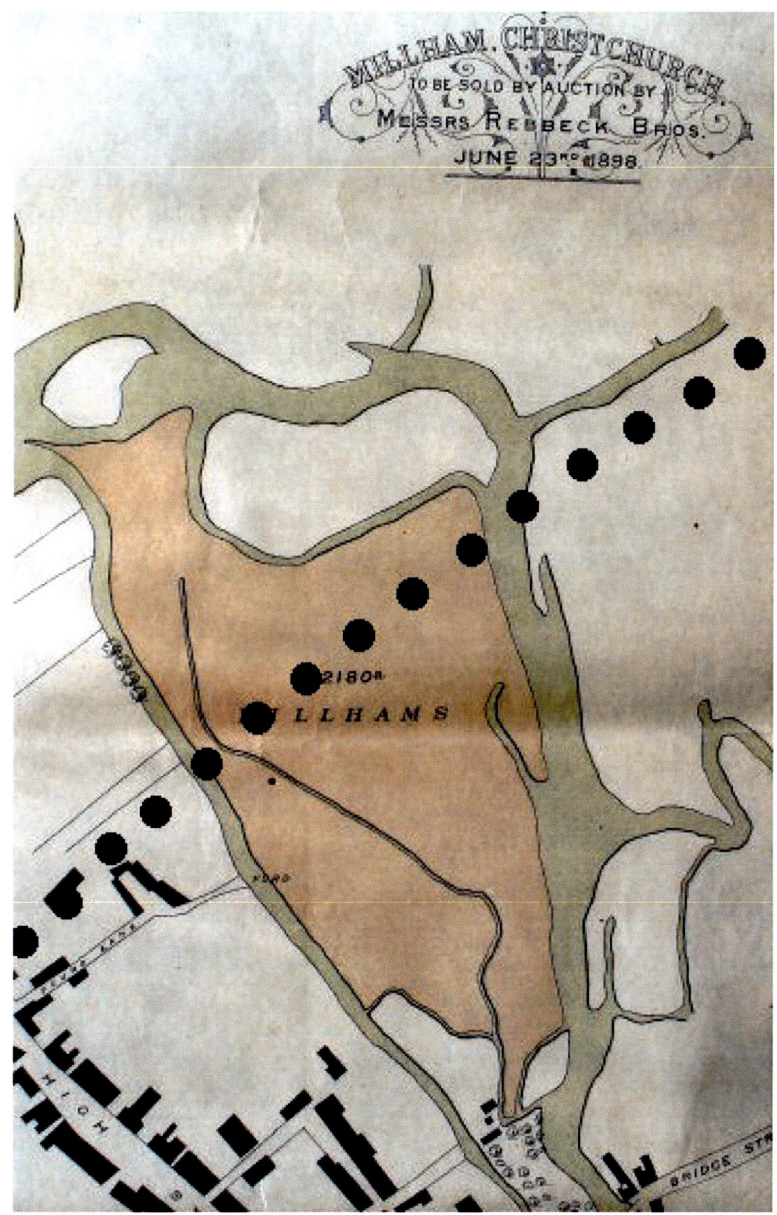

1898 sales plan of Millhams, 60 years before the bypass dissected it (indicated by the dotted line).
Note the ford at Pound Lane. Brewhouse Hole is the area around the most northerly island

Fourteen acres of meadow on the islands between the millstream and the west branch of the Avon; this common was available to the Old Borough inhabitants as an autumn and winter pasture (the aftermath) from Lammas (2 August) through to Candlemas (14 February) and accessed via Pound Lane and Millhams Street over footbridges - simple plank affairs - and the usual gate (mentioned as far back as 1649 in the town documents).

45

When the pasture was open, the owner of the land or its occupier would remove his bridge so that the commoners could place theirs over the millstream, and this process was reversed at the closure.

The use of Millhams as pasture by the commoners appears to have virtually ceased at the outbreak of the Second World War. A fairly lively debate about who was entitled to use this common is recorded in the Coward's Marsh accounts for 1949, in which it was agreed that the stewards should look after the key (indicating the usual locked gate access). It would appear that all persons requiring access were granted their own key. The stewards were not otherwise responsible for Millhams except where problems arose.

As plans for a 'bypass' began to reach fruition soon afterwards, the Commoners' Committee met to debate the issue, and resolved to surrender all rights to the land south of the bypass, and, also unfortunately for history, the commoners' pound, in consideration of the grazing rights of the remaining northern section to be made available for pasturage all the year round, plus an island known as Peggy's Island.

There is documentary evidence for there having been a mill on Little Millhams: the sales particulars above illustrated show part of the presumed mill leat. Another reference in the Hartley Library at Southampton refers to a mill burning down in the 16th century. Access to the mill would probably have been via Ducking Stool Lane. Preliminary investigations to locate the site have commenced.

20th-century view of Barlins in foreground and Millhams (South) in background

Millhams South

Walk (Millhams North)

Nearest car park is the Pit Site. Parking is also available at the Pioneer store (on which site about 30 graves and cremations of pagan Saxon warriors were excavated – see the plaque on the store pillar at the top of the underpass) just off the double dumb-bell roundabout.

Commoners allow free access, but caution is needed when walking on Millhams, and only the section north of the bypass now has any common rights attached to it. Bounded as it is by both the millstream and the Avon, it can become treacherously flooded. Take stout footwear.

Access is from a gate from the end of Beaconsfield Road off lower Bargates. This is at the extreme right of the cul-de-sac, and is very narrow with two steps. The path commences at the bottom of the steps: follow it left. It is restricted in width and when visited on Midsummer's Day 2007, quite overgrown. After a very short distance you will see a lawn mowed right down to the river: this is still the site of the path, so continue, and you will see the wooden footbridge just ahead of you, crossing which will bring you onto North Millhams via a gated entrance (please ensure it is closed after you).

Horses are usually to be found commoned on the pasture, and it is also a popular spot with fishermen, licensed by the Royalty Fisheries whose offices are at the end of Avon Buildings. The whole site abounds with insect life which only unploughed ancient meadow such as this can sustain in abundance: in summer you should see the lovely sight of large groups of brilliant blue darting dragonflies and damselflies, and a rich butterfly population, as well as a good variety of wild flowers which sustains them.

Millhams North: note the unkempt state of the ancient and beautiful millstream.
The 1958 'bypass' is just visible on the right

Close to this spot, you are behind the electricity museum building, a power station constructed in 1905 to power the trams soon to arrive, and you will see a substantial embankment. It may have been a defensive structure to defend the wider town outside of the Bargate (Christchurch was a 10th century burgh, or defended town, with bank and ditch defences). No excavation or other investigation has ever been undertaken on the mound, so its purpose is speculative and its date unknown; what can be said is that it might have continued in a slight curve across Bargates to Barrack Road, from tithe map evidence.

Brewhouse Hole is just beyond the electricity museum — a dangerous whirlpool of water, from which the ancient millstream commences - and may take its name from one of the many beerhouses which proliferated in the town and made their own brew: it is very close to the farm and brewery of Benjamin Baker in upper Bargates. Indeed, there was a brewery on the site of the museum, which may well be the very one; hops have been seen growing close by. A map of c.1720 (by Sir Peter Mews) indicates 'the Wild Weir' near these waters. This was largely dismantled in around 1906, but you can still see, to the right of Brewhouse Hole, a line of ironstones which formed its base.

This weir would have resulted in the raising of the levels of the water in Brewhouse Hole, forcing more water down the millstream to increase its flow dramatically, and thus the turn of the water wheel at Place Mill. A marvellous and previously unknown feat of early civil engineering.

This millstream, flowing under the footbridge, is of unknown date but thought to be of Saxon origin. It was cut to feed the Priory Mill, Place Mill, and on its course passes by the Constable's House, part of Christchurch Castle, where a garderobe (toilet) overhung the waters, so it must have been in a rather polluted state when it reached the mill wheel. Its present overgrown condition is sad to see.

The railway which transverses Millhams was the second to reach the town, being constructed in 1888. This is the main line from London Waterloo to Weymouth.

Proceed to the northerly edge of the common by the Avon River, and cast your eye on the railway line. Looking in the direction of Stoney Lane, you will notice (beyond Millhams North) by the last electricity pylon, a glimpse of a bridge, 'The Three Arches', under the embankment. Binoculars would be helpful here, it has to be said.

On the far side of the branch of the rivulet which these bridges cross, was enacted a famous tragedy.

It was there in 1935 that Alma Rattenbury, a talented and brave lady (awarded the Cross de Guerre in World War One) in her late 30s, plunged a knife six times into her heart and her dead body sank into the whirling waters of the Avon.

What had brought this calamity about? Her jealous lover, George Stoner, had been sentenced to hang for the murder of her elderly husband, a noted architect, at the Rattenbury home in Manor Road, Bournemouth.

Alma had travelled on her release from Pentonville Prison, London, by train to Christchurch. Her last letter, written by the railway bridge crossing the Avon, just to the north-east of the common, expressed deep despair, and that she could not help but feel that the sentence on George was indeed upon herself. She had chosen the spot as it was where George Stoner had told her that he had thought of jumping from the train on his way to his Old Bailey trial.

Alas! By a hideously savage twist of irony, George Stoner's sentence was later commuted to life imprisonment and he served a mere nine years, and survived until 2002. Whatever the rights and wrongs of the tragic outcome for each of the couple, it is quite clear that they genuinely loved one another.

An early July scene in Millhams North

Quomps

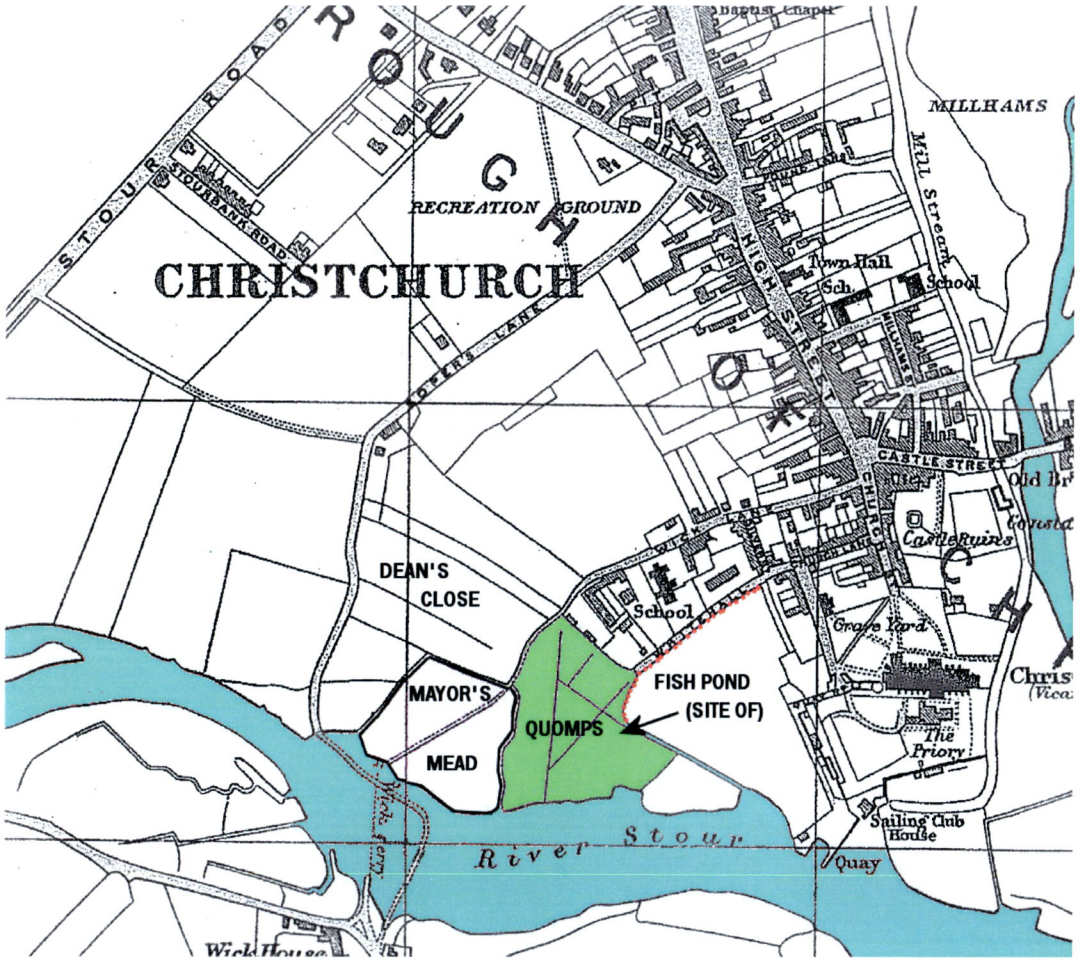

Bright's Map of Bournemouth 1904 indicating the original location of Quomps. The red dotted line shows the site of the wall dividing the two manors, which was removed in the early 20th century

A small meadow pasture of just under five acres alongside the Stour, this was open all year, free of charge to the inhabitants of the Old Borough, another of their 'free commons for ever', which was actually not always free and certainly not for ever, as its present status as recreational open space testifies: not a grazing animal in sight!

The presentments at the Courts Leet were a most necessary procedure: at one time even the priors of the monastery laid a claim to it and even fenced it off in an attempt to enclose it.

Quomps was plainly within the remit of the stewards of Coward's Marsh, as the following entry in their account book in 1765 testifies:

It is hereby agreed by the Mayors, Corporation and Principle [sic] Inhabitants of the Borough of Christchurch, that the Common called Quomps be Hain'd from the 21ˢᵗ of May till the first of July, for ever and every Vote as in Cowards Marsh shall have right to put one Horse or two Cows yet paying one shilling at the Breach . . . That the Common of Quomps from the first of August till the fifteenth of September shall be Hain'd.

Other entries reveal that this common, as with the others, had a gate with a lock to enforce the periods of closure ('haining'), during which the hay would be harvested, and on the breach a similar sense of occasion prevailed as at Coward's Marsh, with the purchase of beer and a payment to the town crier to announce the event. This casts doubt on the common being open all year in practice: it seems to fall a few weeks' short of that claim. A memorandum of the early 19ᵗʰ century refers to the gate as being in Dean's Close. This was one of the closes taken out of Portfield, about which bitter complaint was made. Perhaps it is why the map shows a narrow entrance coming from Wick Lane onto the common. Other account book expenditures were on gravel, which was wheeled onto the swamp (the meaning of the word Quomps) in an effort to raise the ground level.

A note from Lord Malmesbury (Local History Room papers) dated 1935 mentions that the old pronunciation was 'Coom'. Many an enquiry has been made about the meaning of the name Quomps. It would appear to be simply what it was: a swamp or shaky ground.

Separate records for the breach of Quomps survive for two years: 1770 and 1771; the two stewards of Coward's Marsh presenting their accounts on 20 June each year. Twenty-three animals were depastured onto the common in each of those years.

For a period in the 19ᵗʰ century, cricket was played on the common, according to a note in the Red House Museum.

The Lord of one of the two manors (the Borough) who owned Quomps, Lord Malmesbury, in 1909 handed over his rights to the Town Council, on condition that the subsequent use of the ground would be recreational. Sir George Meyrick, as Lord of the other manor concerned (Christchurch-Twyneham), and owner of the Quay, raised no objection. As a matter of interest, Herbert Druitt records the existence of a wall, brick with stone foundations, which used to go down Whitehall then traverse Quomps to demarcate the two manors, destroyed around this time (he remarked in *Christchurch Miscellany* how Christchurch always kills the goose that lays the golden egg).

In 1922 the whole question of its future as a common became the subject of fierce controversy, the council by then having turned the entire area into a rubbish tip and untreated sewage was befouling the river alongside. A pleasant water meadow was being turned into a stinking tip. At an ensuing enquiry no less than 566 signatures were obtained in a protest against the imminent closure: foreshadowing the similar outcry at the perceived threat to Town Common shortly after. The commoners resisted all attempts to part with it and many heated public meetings were held before a compromise could be reached whereby they were financially compensated for the loss of rights. In 1923 the common rights were finally extinguished by these means.

COMMONS ACT, 1899.

INCLOSURE OF QUOMPS COMMON, HANTS

NOTICE IS HEREBY GIVEN, that all persons who claim to have grazing rights in Quomps Common, recently acquired by the Christchurch Town Council under a Closing Order granted by the Ministry of Agriculture and Fisheries, are asked to send in particulars of their CLAIMS to COMPENSATION for the extinguishing of their grazing rights in Quomps Common by the 30th day of June, 1923, to MR. T. BUDDEN, 95, Bargates, Christchurch, Chairman of the Committee appointed by the Commoners. After such date all claims received will be void.

DATED THIS 25TH DAY OF MAY, 1923.

T. BUDDEN   H. DRUITT
J. JENKINS   T. H. McARDLE
W. PAYN

Printed at the Christchurch Times Offices, 5 Bridge Street

Raising the level of Quomps and the Quay and landscaping it to form a pleasure park, together with the consequences of the rubbish accumulation, erased from the map the creek which appears to dissect the two elements of the marshy swamp, as it used to be.

The Quay probably in Victorian times. Place Mill on the left, still a working mill; and Bemister's coal store receiving a delivery of coal from *The Charlotte* on the right. Note the quay's original unmade-up natural state

Walk

Though well known to residents and visitors alike as the heart of the town's beauty spots and events, Quomps as part of the quay nevertheless has points of interest not immediately noticeable. Most convenient car park is Mayor's Mead at the end of Wick Lane.

Enter by the gated access at the end of Church Lane, or by Wick Lane, and proceed past the c.1909 pumping station, which although loathed at the time, standing as it did desolate but prominently amidst a marshy common, is now to be regarded as a handsome and interesting example of Edwardian architecture; a period which particularly relished the use of intricate brick patterns to add interest.

Just beyond this building, as you turn to your left (in the undignified vicinity of the public toilets), you are passing the site of the monastic fishpond for the canons at the Priory, then a monastery. Fish played an important part in the diet in the refectory menus. The pond took advantage of the tidal waters in the harbour to fill and drain it; the same creek may well have served to drain the Castle moat, which casual references describe as draining down onto Quomps.

The bandstand at the eastern end of the quay looks to all the world to be Victorian, yet was the generous gift of a local benefactor in 1937. He wished it to be an anonymous donation to mark the coronation of King George V, but he is now known to have been

David Llewellyn, secretary to the local water board and a man with a huge involvement with charity events, especially the riotous annual carnival.

Close by, at the water's edge, stood a large store for incoming coal. The last barge to operate this trade was called *The Charlotte*. The harbour has never been deep enough to take ships of any size, but was nevertheless the means by which goods would arrive by sea. These would have included the smuggled loads from France and the Channel Islands, a dangerous trade which kept the once poverty-stricken townspeople alive, especially in the 18th century. It was largely suppressed when the Coastguard Service was created in 1832. Christchurch Quay is no longer a commercial quay, except for the tourist boats and café.

From the point at which you can hire a boat, admire the harbour view, with Hengistbury Head in the distance: an Iron-Age and, later, Roman, port trading slaves and dogs for wine. You are standing at the junction of the Stour, coming in from right, and the millstream which feeds Place Mill to your left. This is a building which was traced back by The Society for the Protection of Ancient Buildings as having 12th century foundations, and although the Domesday Book records a mill belonging to the Priory, we cannot be certain, although it is likely, that this was on this exact spot. The mill was mainly used as a corn and then fulling mill, which is a wool process, but the vibration of the machinery caused operations to come to a halt in 1908, and after a long period as a boat store, it was restored and is now a delightful old building to wander around in, and crafts are also sold here. The name almost certainly derives from 'Palace', referring to the conventual Priory, and is recorded in land adjacent: Place Court, for example, the ground between Priory House and the millstream (see the Bulkeley deeds at the Hampshire Record Office).

Take the promenade alongside the river, noticing the Victorian-style street lamps subtly lighting up the pathway, past the rowing club premises and to the car park. This bears the ancient name of Mayor's Mead, and was given to the town by the Aldridge family, but they were not intending it to be tarmaced and used for its current purpose.

Until about the 1980s, a miniature train ran along a set of rails in front of the car park on the grass edge. Sadly missed as it was greatly enjoyed.

The miniature railway

Beyond Mayor's Mead car park, a continuation of Wick Lane leads into what was once the most idyllic spot in Christchurch: Wick Ferry, which for centuries plied its way to the opposite bank at Wick; at first to enable working people to get across the river at that point, it soon became a tourist attraction of enormous popularity, and remains a feature to enjoy even today and use, but its function now is as a leisure attraction.

A lost Christchurch beauty spot – Wick Ferry in its charming heyday, c.1900

Finish your walk with a delightful tea or ice-cream at the tearooms near Place Mill, depicted below, soon after their establishment in the 1920s.

The menu has home-made cakes, cream teas, morning coffee, fruit salad and cream, and prawn teas

Other commons: Stocker's Mead, Bere Mead, Bernard's Mead, Lyte Mead and Gravel Pits

The Pit Site

Dealing with the last one first, as it is the most curious: it was presented at the Court Leet as a matter of routine, but no other reference to this area of the town as common land has been found, except in the statements made by the fire victims of the 1825 disaster on the Pit Site, which destroyed most of the cottages on it. Several people soon after gave evidence to the committee formed to assist those made homeless, that their cottages were built on the land by them or their forefathers without any formal lease, as they considered the land to be theirs as of right, as a common. A few people even disregarded the careful rebuilding scheme which was being painstakingly drawn up, and rebuilt their humble homes to suit themselves, in the same certainty that they had a right to do so. Gravel Pits may, in fact, have formed part of Portfield at one time, but this is speculative: it was clearly not so on the 1844 tithe map, but a most irregular boundary occurs in Portfield at the junction between this and Pit. The name Pit is self-explanatory: the area was exploited for gravel to build the houses which stood on or around it, or perhaps even spread on the extremely muddy roads of the period.

The Pit Site is now a car park and a roundabout, those replacement dwellings of 1825 having become what was considered in the 1950s to be slums, and so cleared.

Walk

It may seem odd to direct the reader's attention to a walk in a car park, but it nevertheless provides interest. It was the most densely populated part of the town until the demolition of its crowded cottages, and contained, besides these, such practical aspects of life as a smithy, wheelwright's shop, and a blind house, or lock-up prison. It also housed a heavy concentration of fusee chain workers once the factory of William Hart was constructed in 1845, and this still survives and is visible from the Pit Site at the bottom end of Bargates. Female and child (and a few adult males') labour was employed at the factory and in their cottages on the processes involved in manufacturing these minute watch-regulating chains: riveters, wire cutters, hookmaking and so on. Looking towards Bargates, close to the roundabout, may be seen the memorial horse trough erected as a tribute to Samuel Bemister, seven times mayor of the town. It used to have a water supply at its base for passing dogs to partake of refreshment.

There was a mid-19th century public house at the apex of Bargates and Barrack Road, on a site now under the roundabout. Called the Antelope, it had a distinctive replica of that animal projecting high up on the Bargates side. The surviving public house on Barrack Road, The Duke of Wellington, had a brewery range behind it. The Pit Site was once a raucous and rowdy part of the town, scene of many drunken fights and women's squabbles: a little hard to recreate in the imagination from the current use.

The small and now near derelict building next to this pub was close to the former town fire station (since demolished) – quite ironically, in view of the devastation by fire to the original cottages in 1825, in which some 55 people were made homeless. The stone plaque created to commemorate the fire, and which was once affixed to one of the rebuilt cottages, may be seen at the Red House Museum.

Other Commons

The other lesser commons were of the 'aftermath' type, basically river meadows which are highly fertile on account of regularly being inundated by the river floodwater bearing rich silt, and were derived from a charter of Baldwin de Redvers. Other lands included in this grant of privileges were Mayor's Mead (now Quomps car park), The Halves (in Stanpit, also known as Mayor's Acre), and The Butts, which are now in the proximity of the flowerbeds on the town recreation ground, near Magdalen Lane. This grant gave the Corporation (i.e. the mayor and burgesses) the right to pasture after the first crop had been harvested, for a fee.

On 17 October 1636, the town documents note that: '*It has been agreed that 18d a cow be paid for the Rent of Stockers Mead and Bernards Mead by those that have the pasture with commons which comes to £3 to be equally divided amongst the burgesses*'.

The practice was to let these lands and use the money to pay the Lord of the Manor and repair town property, such as gates, banks, ditches, shops, the Town Hall and other expenses of the Corporation.

Stocker's Mead

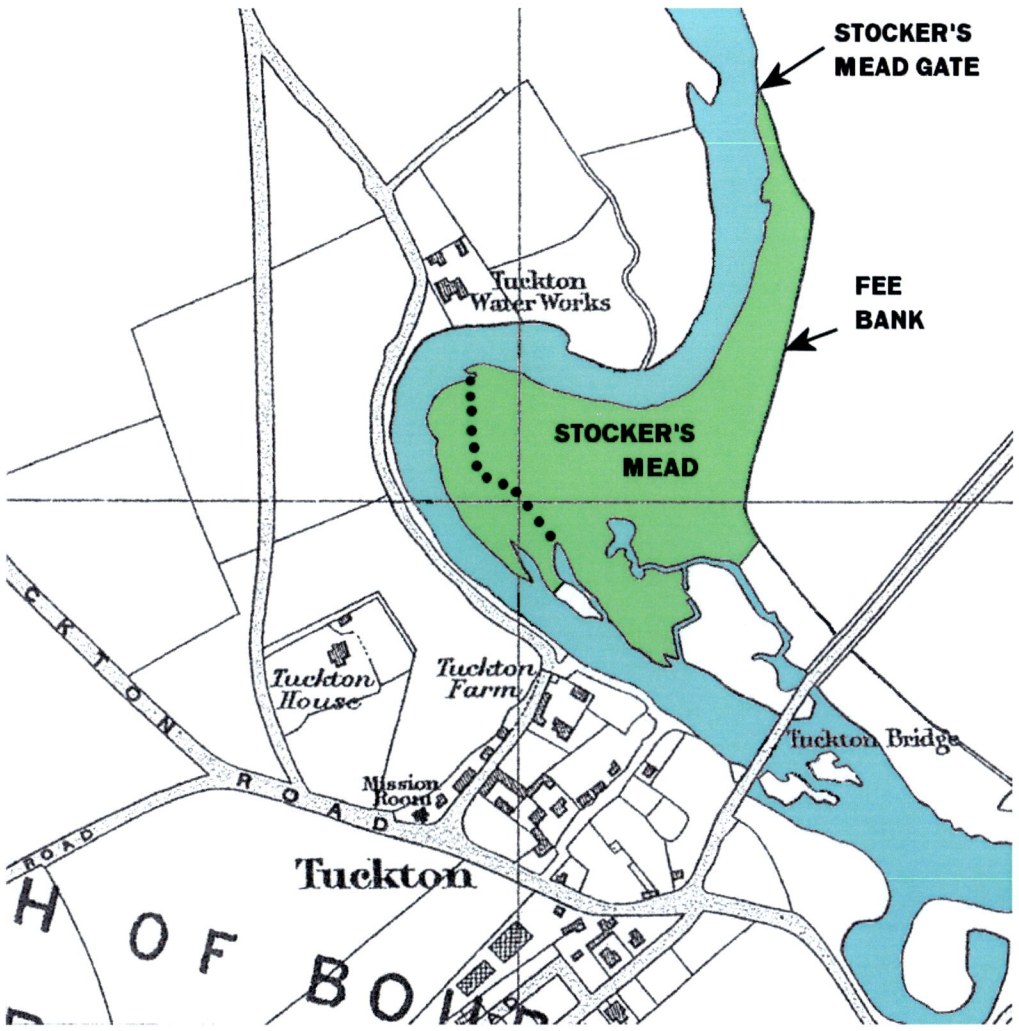

Bright's Map of Bournemouth 1904 modified to show the boundary of Stocker's Mead,
the area known as Constable's Acre (dotted line demarcates this), Fee Bank, and the ford incorporating
a track called Tuckton Road

Stocker's Mead used to have a gate to its entrance: this is shown on the modified extract of the Portfield map on page 37 and its position is clearly marked in the photograph adjacent where the tarmac path merges into the gravel raised walk.

This elevated walk is the most remarkable feature to survive in Stocker's Mead: the Fee Bank is a raised structure which an anonymous memorandum in the Druitt Collection of the 19th century describes as '*a road from Priory to Iford; from a quantity of rubble and loose stones found in the centre supposed to originally [be] a Roman road*'.

Site of Stocker's Mead Gate

Certainly, a map schedule of 1796 in the Hampshire Record Office refers to it a as '*a Bank on which the Monks used to walk. It continues to the Church*'. This suggests a way of some antiquity, as well as being a boundary between Stocker's Mead and Portfield. It is clearly visible as a raised bank in the photograph on page 61.

Stocker's Mead was the scene of the worst known outbreak of commons disputes, but on this occasion, of such a violent nature that the prolonged repercussions would have shaken the town, seriously challenged the authority of the mayor and burgesses, and sent waves of terror into the hearts of the other commoners, some of whom feared for their lives.

It is a story from the Elizabethan era, and the perpetrator – who appears to have had some serious anger management issues or was actually a psychopath – was one William Osborne, who hailed from Fordingbridge.

Ruthless, determined and savage, William Osborne was convinced that the aftershare of several acres, and a ham, in the mead belonged to him, i.e. after the hay had been cut. Every year since Baldwin de Redvers had made the grant of the land to the mayor and burgesses (the 'Old Corporation'), they paid an annual rent to the lord of the castle of the town (in other words, to the Lord of the Manor of Christchurch). However, about 1490, the Earl of Huntingdon as Lord of the Manor, had sold a tenement and this ham, plus eight acres of Stocker's Mead, and it descended to a William Ballye, alias Jumper, who died in 1571. So often the name Jumpers is incorrectly thought to derive from 'juniper', but there was an actual family of this name in the town in this period.

Fee Bank, plainly visible as a raised embankment

The property became Osborne's, probably by inheritance, and he certainly believed he was entitled to it, yet the mayor and burgesses had been utilising the aftershare of his property. He appeared to be in the right: he went to court (the Andover Assizes) and the judgement was in his favour. The original grant was unclear about the rights, but it had been customary only to interpret them as referring to the foreshare, the aftershare remaining with the Lord of the Manor. Osborne thought differently and in the years which led up to his increasingly 'vexatious' behaviour he had been in litigation with several burgesses in other disputes over entitlement to Stocker's Mead. It would appear that the Earl of Huntingdon had no right to have sold pieces of the common back in the 15th century.

At one point, the inhabitants had been aggrieved enough to petition the Lords of the Assizes, because Osborne had been bound over for good behaviour but this had not stopped further 'vexatious' actions from him which culminated in him shooting and wounding one William Pope who was attending to his cattle.

Moreover, as the Andover trial was going on, Osborne had put some hay on the ham, almost certainly provocatively, which the burgesses' cattle naturally wandered up to and ate. Retaliation was swift: Osborne drew his sword and cruelly and fatally wounded three of the offending cattle in 1591. This showed the man's true colours. Not satisfied with that, he issued a writ against one of the burgesses whose bullock he had stabbed to death – and won his case for damages! But it was done, it was claimed, by Osborne lying to the Sheriff. After his successful case, Osborne has escalated the antagonism to several attempts of murder. It did not help that some burgesses kept breaking the lock into Stocker's Mead, and entering into it, fully armed – sometimes in the night. Osborne was convinced that they had found his title documents there (he having unaccountably brought them into the field, and even more unaccountably lost what must have been sizeable parchment rolls).

In 1592, one of his antagonists, Thomas Hancock, was actually jailed at Winchester pending further legal action against him by Osborne, preparatory to an appearance before the Queen's Court at Hertford Castle. Another, William Nutkyns, summoned to appear at Hertford Castle, had begged, borrowed and sold his belongings to finance the appearance. His widow poignantly wrote, explaining his non-appearance, that her husband had told her that the stress of the accusations would be the death of him, and it was, leaving her a 'poor widow'.

Fresh from his latest battle of wills with the burgesses, Osborne requested a lease of Stocker's Mead aftershare, but this was refused on account of his disgraceful conduct. It may be courageous but not necessarily wise to defy such a man as Osborne. He vowed he would make the burgesses repent their refusal.

The case was destined to reach the Star Chamber, but the current Earl of Huntingdon appears to have defused the situation by granting him a lease to the land in question for 21 years, and the uproar died down. Maybe the case died with him before the lease was up. Osborne was a known trouble-maker in his home town too, but in some ways his arguments were, though vindictive in motive, useful in exposing the rather shaky foundations on which the entitlement to the rights of commons rested.

And the burgesses were quite capable of swindling when it suited them too: vis-à-vis the closes, or enclosures, these powerful people appropriated from the various commons, fencing them against other users.

As long ago as 1566, the Court of Exchequer, acting for Queen Elizabeth as the then holder of Bere Mead, Stocker's Mead and Bernard's Mead, took action against certain powerful Christchurch inhabitants, who had simply seized all these commons and prevented anyone else using them – by force! They were not, it seemed, even burgesses but had merely pretended to be, to justify their pocketing of the profits. Utterly chaotic and quite lawless behaviour. One of those people cited, John Pawson, was also a burgess during the 'Osborne Outrage'; one assumes 25 years later he was the same man but sons often took their fathers' names. Dashwin's Close was another ancient enclosure out of the western side of Stocker's Mead (document collection D/RHM at the Dorset Record Office). This quotes from 'a conversation at Court Leet':

Juryman to Town Clerk and Corporation present: 'Please where is Dashwin's Close?'. Town Clerk: 'What business is that of yours?' Juryman: 'I wanted to know before I was sworn.' 'What business is it to you more than any other juryman?' Mr Buffet had been summoned as a juryman and hearing this answer given he said, 'Then, gentlemen, I will not be sworn', and he was walking away when the Town Clerk said he should fine him. He asked what was the fine. '3s 6d' was the reply. Mr Buffet paid it and left without being sworn.

What an indictment to the way the Corporation used and abused its powers and privileges. The name Buffet suggests an early Victorian date for this recollection, which at least showed someone in the town had some principles when it came to common land and the ever-proffered open hand. But . . .

Blood on the commons. Dead cattle. A wounded commoner. Attempted murder. A jailed burgess. The commons were, quite literally, held so dear and were so valued as to be fought over, on their soil or by legal action or by stealth.

In more modern times, the concept of the aftershare became quite incompatible with land use, and so the aftershare of Stocker's Mead was exchanged for some land in the recreation ground with the owner of the foreshare, Sir William Rose. Thus the entire pasture became available year-round for the inhabitants. It remains public open space.

Walk

Access to Stocker's Mead may be gained from The Meridians. There is a small car park off Wentworth Drive, which if used, you will need to turn right to get back to the beginning of the walk. Follow the curve of the road as far as its final right-hand bend, at which you will notice a footpath on the left signposted as such. Follow this long tarmac path until it opens out onto the large expanse of land, with the river plainly visible in front of you. You will be standing next to a lamp-post where you will notice that the tarmac has ended. You are standing on the original site of Stocker's Mead Gate.

Proceed along the raised Fee Bank, and take any one of a number of pathways which branch off as the bank peters out. Ramble where you wish amongst the lush meadow vegetation, but notice the sharp bend in the river, where you can see the riverside houses of Tuckton across the water. In that protective curve was carved out a reserved piece of land, known on the 1796 map schedule as Constable's or Lord's Acre (it is more than an acre). Bearing in mind that the Fee Bank probably belonged to the canons of the Priory, it is interesting to speculate whether this piece of land was reserved for another exalted owner's exclusive use: the Lord of the Manor, who owned the castle in the town, and we can still boast of the Constable's House from the 12th century surviving. Perhaps this piece was flooded regularly and so enriched with nutrients as a result that it was reserved for the use of the Lord's constable.

As you proceed and look westwards across the river, you will see the old pumping station across the wide stretch of the Stour at this point. Now converted, this building (pictured) had a most notable history, in being the site in Edwardian times of the printing works of the Russian writer, Count Tolstoy, smuggled out of his home country where his works were banned by the Tsarist regime, and printed here by a small but locally well-known band of Russian exiles, led by a Count Tcherktoff, Tolstoy's agent. The books were then smuggled back into Russia.

Tuckton Pumping Station (left)

Bere Mead

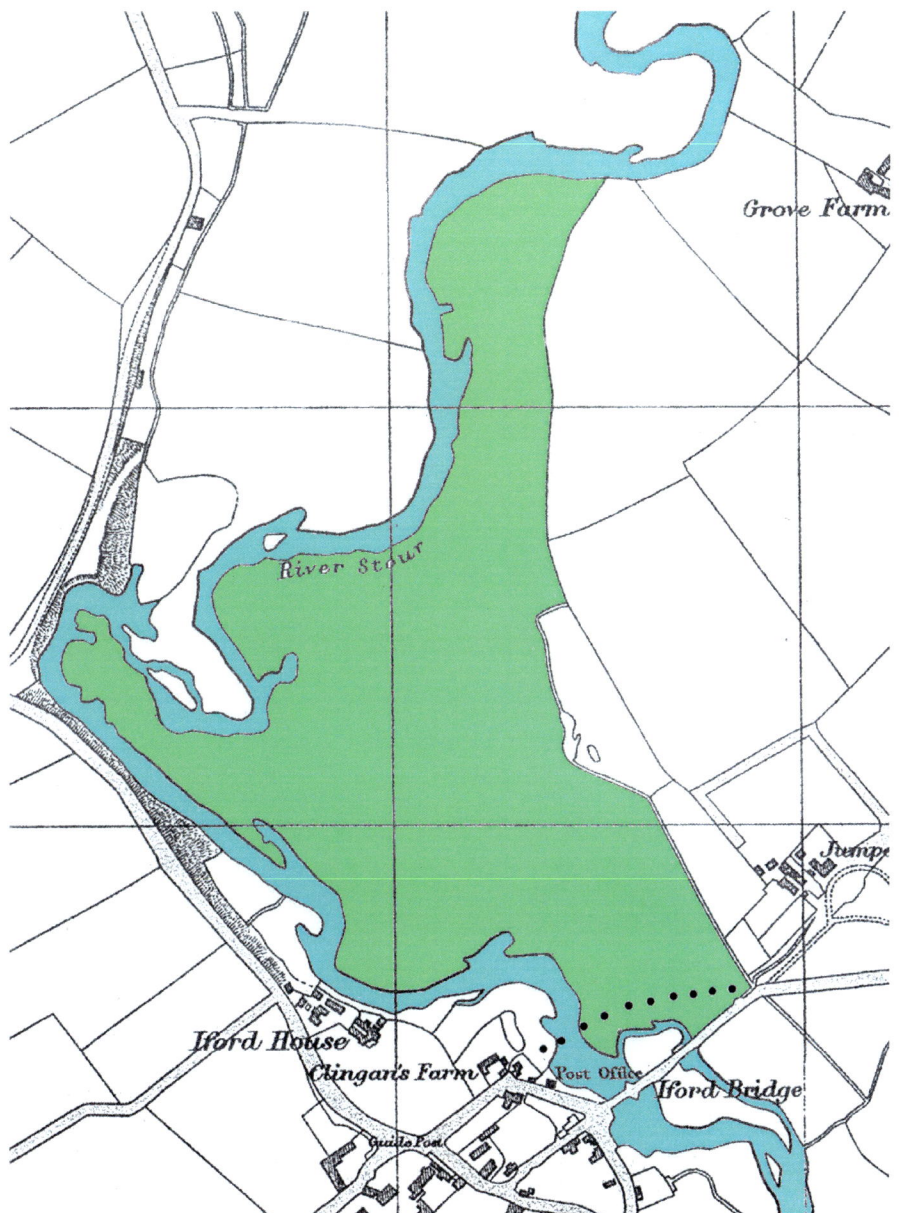

Bright's Map of Bournemouth, 1904, coloured to show the boundary of Bere Mead

Bere (or Bure) Mead was available to the Corporation at a cost of 12d per beast and was acknowledged to provide enough pasture for 200 sheep – intensive use. It appears to be contiguous to Bernard's Mead, separated only by Iford Bridge, suggesting the possibility that before the bridge was constructed (as far as we know, in Norman times), Bere and Bernard's Mead were one common.

A document, undated, but probably 17th century (Local History Room), refers to 'a certain wrong', enacted by named individuals, depriving once again the ordinary townsperson from exercising their common rights – it may be connected to the deranged saga described within the Stocker's Mead section.

The same document proves that Bere Mead was also fenced and/or hedged and ditched, as the other burgesses' commons were. It was again available for the herbage between Lammas and Candlemas.

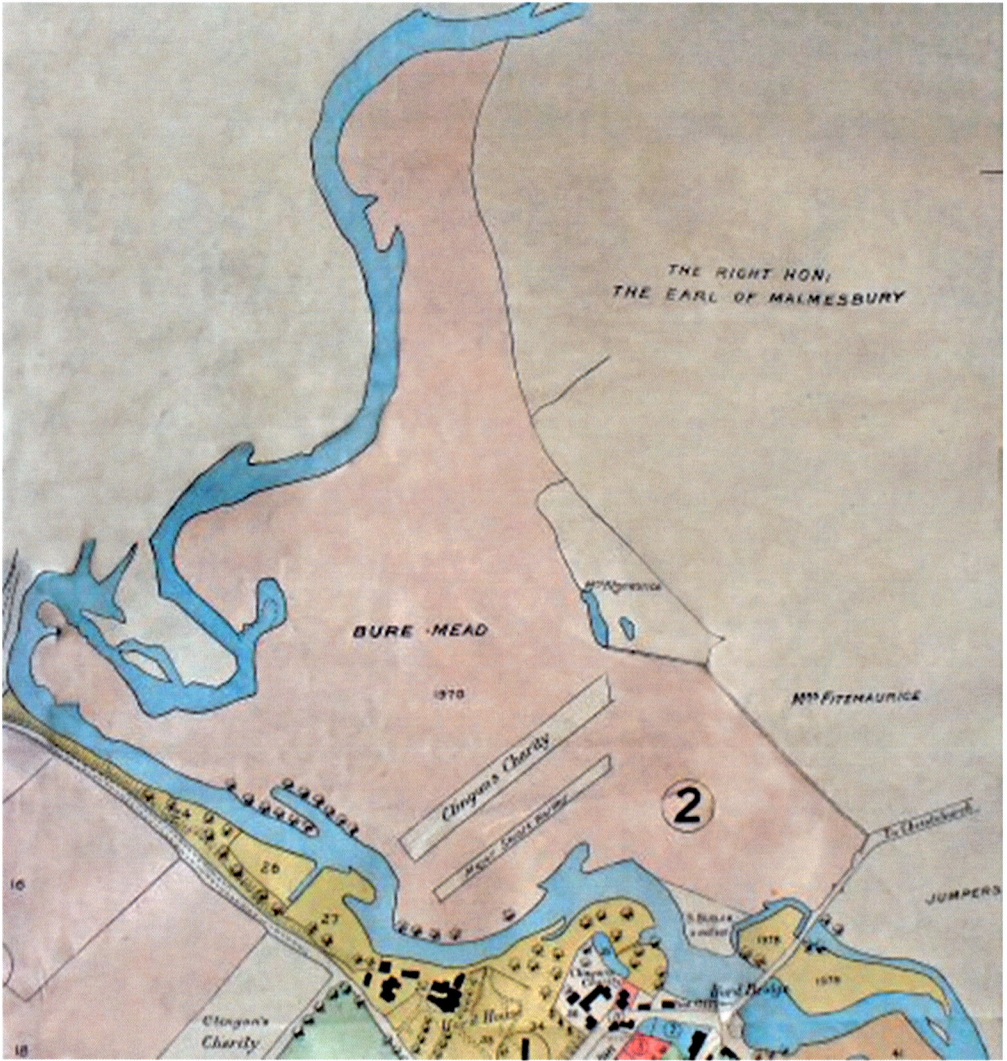

Bere (Bure) Mead: 1898 sales plan

The map above includes a detailed plan of Iford village and house, and also a strip of land within Bere Mead assigned to Clingan's Charity. Bure Mead contained 47 acres.

From 1898 sales particulars, entitled 'Part of Bure Mead with the Stour and Grounds of Iford House'. Iford Bridge is visible in the distance

Modern-day view of Iford Golf Course: the clubhouse is just on the horizon on the right

That it is shown as a strip suggests this mead was allocated in strips, as were Ogber and Portfield. The charity book commenced in 1737, by the will of John Clingan, who wished to provide an apprenticeship scheme for the poor of the parish. The remarkable document of the parish poor apprenticed survives (Christchurch Library Local History Room), providing a rich source for social and family history. The trades involved can be traced from cordwainers (shoemakers), staymakers and glovers, through 'pericle' (wig) makers and mantua (ladies' cloaks) makers, through to hairdressers and tailors.

Bere Mead is now converted to a surprising and rather incongruous new use, as Iford Golf Course, with a clubhouse, and blindingly illuminated at night. The only walkers to avail themselves of it now are members of the golf club.

Bernard's Mead

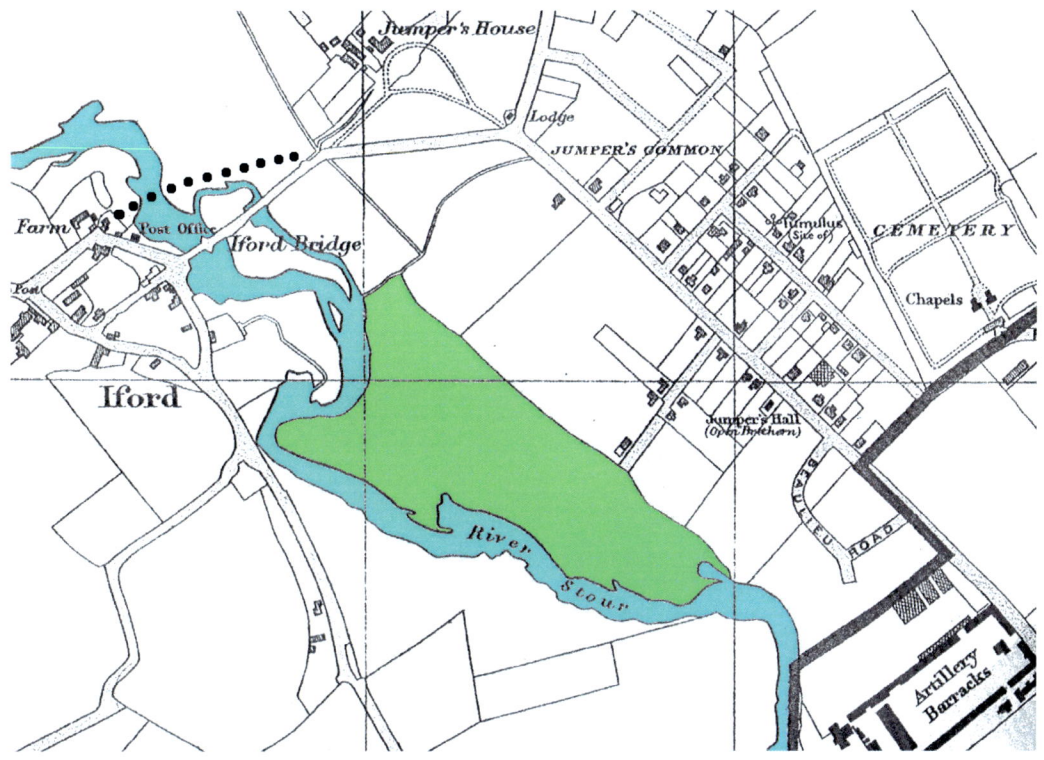

Bright's map of Bournemouth 1904 modified to show the boundary as of the 1844 tithe map. The piece south of Iford Bridge is now considered part of Bernard's Mead but is not included as such in the tithe map. The dotted line represents the 1934 Barrack Road diversion

This common had several owners and several occupiers. References in old documents are scanty, but the following appears in the Mayor's Accounts of October 1658: *'To Richard Fflorry for loading a frith at Bernards Mead, 2s 6d'*.

Bernard's Mead was again subject to an exchange of rights, which in this case took place in 1925, allowing all-year round use to the inhabitants on condition that the land was used for recreation and a riverside walk. The foreshare was the hay crop, and the aftershare for beasts to consume what was left from the crop, or its regrowth. Pasture rights date back to the 12th or 13th century – an incredible length of time. Returning to 1925, a Mr A E Shave then owned it, and seven acres of foreshore were exchanged for two of the aftershare.

Of all the burgesses' commons, it was by far the largest. It fell victim to the usual indignity meted out to the town commons, being filled up with rubbish between the wars. Soon after the last war the Council attempted to turn it into a holiday camp, a move which engendered a prolonged legal battle which the Council lost on account of the 1925 covenant.

There is, nevertheless, a holiday camp occupying the eastern end of the former common, so how and why and when this arrived is a matter of speculation.

Undated postcard from authors' collection

Eastern end of Bernard's Mead

Walk

Part of the flood defence system of the end of the last century crosses and bisects Bernard's Mead now, so its use for fairs, circuses and other events is no longer possible. Nevertheless, it is a beautiful and quite extensive riverside walk, accessed from Barrack Road by the end of the flood embankment or from nearby Maundeville Crescent.

Bernard's Mead has the merit of being bounded by the ancient Iford Bridge, dating back many hundreds of years, probably from Norman times and certainly one was recorded in 1140, but in its present form rebuilt in 1784 by the county (Hampshire) which was responsible for its upkeep, and by G G Hookey in particular.

It had only two spans and was a single-track bridge with passing bays. Reference is made (Marjorie P Lane) to the difficulties faced by heavily-laden horse traffic on the bridge in the nineteenth century; also of a team of oxen pulling a load of cheeses stacked spectacularly high: so much so that this vast cavalcade had to be preceded by a man blowing a horn to warn oncoming traffic that the bridge was blocked.

Iford Bridge, viewed from Bernard's Mead

By 1832 Iford Bridge had fourteen arches, but two spans were removed in 1932 when Barrack Road was diverted to its current path. The bridge was strenuously fought for, as it was going to be entirely demolished by the Hampshire County Council, which relented under the pressure. Enjoy walking across this ancient bridge, with its projecting passing places.

71

On the opposite bank of the Stour you could once have looked across at a hamlet of thatched cottages – the old village of Iford, eradicated in the early 20th century for suburban houses, so totally it is as if it had never existed, alongside its grand house of 1826, Iford House, home to the Farr family who had parliamentary connections in the 18th century. Now a band of mature trees completely obscures the Bournemouth (as it is now) side of the Stour.

Over that side was a landing stage, where the ground sloped gently to the river at which point it was a mere two feet deep. This edge was railed for safety around 1900 on account of a horse, no doubt refreshing itself but, happening to be attached to a cart with a driver, had gone into the water too far and been swept away and drowned. Nevertheless, this access to water was regularly used by local horse traffic and cattle. Remarkably, the cavalcade of thirsty animals using this drinking stop on at least one occasion included elephants, part of a travelling circus going from Christchurch to Pokesdown via Iford Bridge; and a pair of long-horned bullocks which drew a covered wagon of suet! Steam-driven vehicles would also pause for refilling at this point, both farm machines and fair machines.

View from Iford Bridge, c.1900.
Note the railed-off watering hole with
Iford village behind

Lyte Mead

Last and, it has to be said, least, Lyte Mead appears to have been an encroachment from Portfield, and the same anonymous memorandum (previously quoted) notes that the owner, Mr [James] Druitt, 'unjustly ploughed [it]'. Resentment again from the commoners against any tampering with their commons.

To Conclude

Throughout the many centuries, the common lands of the town have proved of such inestimable worth to the poorer inhabitants that any threat to the continuation of the ancient rights associated with them produced fierce resistance, mass opposition and legal and even physical challenges. This reaction has persisted well into modern times, as witnessed by the Bernard's Mead fiasco of half a century ago and within the last decade the attempt to turn Barrack Road Recreation Ground into an eventing arena - as with the Bernard's Mead caravan park, an ill-judged and unlawful attempt to enclose the common for commercial gain for the 'corporation'. Enclosure brings with it the abolition of rights: Quomps has been lost as common land but arguably all the residents and visitors benefit from its new status as a riverside amenity; Portfield is lost but the town has been able to expand by its development. Town Common remains a common but has been opened up to all. So long as *historic* rights are safeguarded, advantage can be gained from abolition of the *common* rights, so long as the end result makes the land available to all, at no cost, and is not exploited for gain.

Coward's Marsh and Ogber live and thrive in the 21st century, carefully managed by its stewards and the herdsman as it always was, together with a dedicated commoners' committee. We owe a debt to the past commoners for the preservation of these remaining open spaces in present times, providing essential green lungs in an otherwise heavily developed modern borough.

We must use or lose them: '**our free commons** *forever*'.

Stocker's Mead in spring

Final word: look at the beauty of the commons walks.

Enjoy!

Bibliography

Barnes, Frederick W: *Iford, the Lost Village*; Bournemouth Local Studies, n.d.

Bremner, Sylvia, and Hughes, Michael (editors): The South Hampshire Archaeological Rescue Group: *Rescue Archaeology in Hampshire*; Number 3, 1975

Druitt, Herbert: *Christchurch Miscellany*, first published c.1919-1930 in the parish magazine

Druitt, Herbert: Report on the Records of the Borough of Christchurch-Twyneham (Christchurch Library Local History Room, ref 12-2-50)

Druitt, Herbert: *The Book of Bournemouth*, 1934

Jarvis, Keith S: Excavations in Christchurch 1969-1980

Lane, Marjorie P: *Christchurch*, c.1960

Newman, Sue: *The Christchurch and Bournemouth Union Workhouse*, second edition, 2000

Newman, Sue and Tizzard, Mike, for The Christchurch Local History Society: *Millennium Trail* leaflet

Starks, Robert: *Reflections and Recollections of Christchurch and Locality*. 2000

Woodhead, Felicity: *Flora of the Christchurch Area*, 1994

The Christchurch Times

Various single documents from both the Hampshire and Dorset Record Offices and the Red House Museum

The Town Documents: the deeds of the property of the Old Corporation of Christchurch

The Tithe Map for Christchurch, 1844, and schedule

Papers in the personal collections of the authors

The Hampshire Repository, 1801